HUGH JOHNSON

Wine Journal

First published in 2011 by Mitchell Beazley, an imprint of Octopus Publishing
Group Ltd, Endeavour House, 189 Shaftesbury Avenue, London WC2H 8JY
www.octopusbooks.co.uk

www.octobusbooksusa.com

An Hachette UK Company www.hachette.co.uk

Distributed in the US by Hachette Book Group USA, 237 Park Avenue

New York NY 10017 USA

Distributed in Canada by Canadian Manda Group, 165 Dufferin Street

Toronto, Ontario, Canada M6K 3H6

Editor Alex Stetter

Editorial Director Tracey Smith

Consultant Margaret Rand

Art director Jonathan Christie

Design & art direction Yasia Williams-Leedham

Production manager Peter Hunt

ISBN: 978 1 84533 603 5

Printed and bound in Italy

HUGH JOHNSON

Wine Journal

MITCHELL BEAZLEY

Contents

How to use this journal

Wine needs words.

At least that's my contention. Words to identify. Words to discuss. Words to record.

Here are some of mine, mainly on the practical aspects of what (I'm forced to admit) is quite a complicated subject. And space for some of yours ...

Writing notes is how I remember when, where and (very important) with whom I drank my favourite bottles. As to describing them ... that's always a struggle.

Choosing wine

When your mind starts to turn towards an evening glass of wine, how does the prospect present itself to you? Is your first concern the odds of a heart attack, and the golden opportunity of lengthening them by a microfraction if you choose red rather than white? Neither is mine.

Who do I consult? My companions. My dinner prospects. My tasting duties. My bank balance. Most powerfully, though least palpably, the crystallising image of thirst, the anticipation of winey pleasure, forming in my mind as evening approaches. It is, strange to say, quite specific.

The funny thing is that it rarely, if ever, forms itself into the thought 'I feel like a Cabernet'. Or a Merlot, a Syrah, or even a Pinot Noir. (My subconscious doesn't really do varietals at all. I think places, countries, regions, growers, vineyards. I think sweetness, fruity uplift, gripping tannins, scouring acidity or inspiring bubbles before I think grapes.)

There is a list of wine flavours in my unconscious, just as there is a food menu. You are just the same: lamb, fruit, an egg, salmon, a jam sandwich are all there in your mental menu. For one reason or another (you may even believe it is your body chemistry issuing instructions) one or other takes priority and becomes what you want. The wine I want, in this first recognition of specific thirst, is almost always white.

Bruno Prats once memorably said that white wine is what you drink before

When choosing wine, I consult the anticipation of winey pleasure, forming in my mind as evening approaches.

you drink red wine. I would put it the other way round. More and more I find that we use Riesling or Silvaner or Pinot Blanc (either German or from Alsace, but more often German) to open the session: a glass before dinner while we bustle round the kitchen, then probably another with some fishy or meaty appetizer. People tend to react to Riesling as though finding food to match it is a puzzle. In a recent *Harpers* supplement (*Harpers* is the increasingly lively wine trade organ) trendy chefs were thinking of daft things to do with Riesling: throwing soy sauce and ginger at it, for heaven's sake. Have they forgotten (or not been told) that it is the perfect match for almost all sorts of cold meat? Charcuterie is an irresistible accompaniment. Cold game birds (as a rule tastier than hot) are never better than with a crisp Spätlese.

Judy and I then often leave bottle A in the fridge for the next evening and move on to bottle B for the main course, which as often as possible is fish, hard as it is to come by out here in the country. We'd be sunk without our deep freeze. Out comes another bottle of

white wine: usually something of more weight and substance – even Chardonnay. We are Chablis freaks, but a bit of everything crosses the Johnson threshold.

And red wine? It is always the centrepiece of a dinner party, but alone at home we find that it makes the perfect contemplative sipping when thirst has been quenched, with a book by the fireside.

Taking notes

I try to have an annual health check of my drinking habits, to see whether they change (not greatly) and whether they reflect the recorded trends of wine-drinking Britain at large (they don't). The scarcely scientific base I use is the black tasting book I've been keeping in my kitchen for countless years. What gets into it are wines that are new to me, or have developed since I last drank them, and that make an impression on me that I think worth recording. My default wines, Chablis and claret from the family bin, are not normally counted.

Judy and I are not always in the kitchen. We travel. We spend time in London. We even get asked out. I go to tastings: these are not part of this count. The count of recorded 'with-supper wines' in the past year totals 206. Of these, 57 are reds from France, 30 whites from Germany, 30 whites from France, 21 different Champagnes. Then come Australia with 11, Eastern Europe with ten, Italy with nine, fortified wines (Port, Sherry and similar) with nine, Spain with six, South America five, California and New Zealand both with four,

England three, 'Other European' three, South Africa and Portugal both with two.

Certainly the raw figures surprise me. Do I really drink more German wine than French? I am always trying a new Mosel Kabinett or Spätlese, it's true. In summer they almost have soft-drink status here, having something like half the alcohol content of a Chardonnay from the southern or western hemisphere. The endless expressiveness of Riesling nearly always makes them seem worth a note in the book.

Nine seems a very low figure for Italy, too. I tend to let my Italian wines hang until they are a bit gamey, like the Castello di Brolio Chianti Classico 1997 of the other night. It was a surprisingly deep red, with that thrilling sharp/sour/gritty nose of mature Sangiovese. There was still lots of red vinosity, just giving way in the finish to appetising asperity. Chianti, and the truly claret bend from San Leonardo in the Trentino, are perpetual favourites; true food wines.

The real interest of the notebooks for me, naturally enough, is the notes. How many lines of description I write about each entry is much more revealing than a score out of three, five, seven, 20 or 100. There are wines I sum up simply with a joyful cry of recognition (or a harrumph). There are others where a fairly formal note – colour, smell, flavours, finish – seems to say it all. And there are a few, every couple of pages, where I scribble and scribble, learning more from each visit to the glass, hoarding a drop to keep sniffing back at my desk or over *Newsnight*.

Length of note equates to measure of interest. Any wine can end with an exclamation mark. Really good ones end with a string of questions.

There are wines I sum up simply with a joyful cry of recognition (or a harrumph).

Enjoying wine

It is the inquisitive who enjoy wine most. The essence of the game is variety; you could taste a different wine every day of your life and yet not learn it all. Each wine evolves with time. There will always be new wines to taste, and new combinations of wine with food to try. There will also always be more to learn about yourself, your palate, and its reactions.

No single attitude or set of rules can apply to a commodity that can be either a simple foodstuff as basic as bread and cheese, or one of the most recherché of luxuries, or anywhere in between. There are enamel-mug wines and Baccarat-crystal wines, and there is no point in pretending that one is the other.

The next pages are concerned with choosing, buying, storing, serving, and appreciating wine that is above the *ordinaire* or jug level. Once a wine has a named origin (as opposed to being an anonymous blend) it reflects a particular soil, climate, culture, and tradition. For better or worse, the wine then has some character. The mastery of wine consists in recognising, bringing out, and making the most of that character. I cannot improve on the late André Simon's definition of a connoisseur: 'One who knows good wine from bad, and appreciates the distinctive merits of different wines.' Thank heaven all white wines are not Sauvignon Blancs, however fresh, flowery, and fragrant, or all reds great thumping Cabernets. It

you could taste a different wine every day of your life and yet not learn it all.

is a crucial (but also a common) misunderstanding of the nature and variety of wine to say that a Barolo, for example, is better than a Rioja, or a Pauillac than a Napa Cabernet. The secret is to learn to understand and enjoy each of them for what they are.

There is only one essential I would press on you, if you are going to spend more than a bare minimum and buy wines above the jug level: and that is to make a conscious act of tasting. Become aware of the messages your nose and mouth are sending you – not just about wine, but about all food and drink. Seek out new tastes and think about them.

By far the greater part of all fine wine, and even – perhaps especially – of the best, is thrown away by being used as a mere drink. A great bottle of wine is certainly wasted if nobody talks about it, or at least tries to pinpoint in his or her own consciousness the wonderful will-o'-the-wisp of fragrance and flavour.

Buying wine

To buy wine and get exactly what you expect is the exception rather than the rule. Wine is a moving target: a kaleidoscope of growers and vintages that never stands still. If this bothers you, there is a solution – stick to a brand, since the whole point of a brand is to deliver unvarying flavour and style. But you will be sacrificing the great fascination of wine, its infinite variety, not to mention the fun of the chase: the satisfaction of finding a winner (and the chagrin of backing a dud).

There are few cardinal rules in such an open field, where one day you may be buying from the corner store, the next by mail order, and the third direct from the producer. But it is certainly better to think carefully about what you want to buy before you buy it. Sometimes, of course, you will just want a decent bottle to accompany a dish you are preparing for guests that very day, but whenever possible, buy ahead of your needs.

Nobody can take in all the offerings of a well-stocked store at a glance. Do your wine buying when you are in the mood and have time to browse, to compare prices, to make calculations, to use reference books. By far the best place to do this is at home, by comparing the price lists of alternative suppliers. Given time you can make an order that qualifies for a discount. Buying by the case, even the mixed case, is invariably cheaper

Wine is a moving target: a kaleidoscope of growers and vintages that never stands still.

than buying by the bottle. Keep an eye out for 'bin-end sales', usually held in January, when all the top merchants send out lists of discounted wines, either because they are overstocked or because they are moving on to a new vintage. Although you should take care not to buy a tired wine that's in decline, such lists often contain wonderful mature German wines or vintage ports from lesser-known shippers, and many other bargains.

A fine wine needs time to rest. Although many modern whites and light reds are so stable that you could play skittles with them and do them no harm, mature red wines need to settle for at least several days after being moved. Your chances of serving a wine at its best are far greater if you can prepare it calmly at home.

In the past, wine-buyers had to rely on either their own knowledge and experience or those of their wine merchant. Today there are many more ways to acquire information, such as the websites of wine producers. These sites vary in quality, but most give detailed information about the range and styles of wines produced, and provide email addresses so that, should you wish, you can obtain further information from that producer. Moreover, there are many websites and blogs that specialise in providing information to consumers in the form of tasting notes, vintage notes, news about changes in the industry, and so forth. These sites may or may not be linked to sites selling wine. Some of the more rarefied and detailed wine websites are pay sites; many others are free.

Investing in pleasure

An investment in future pleasure is often one of the most profitable of all. Inflation aside, when you come to drink the wine, now better than when you bought it, the expenditure will be a thing of the past; the pleasure will seem a gift from the gods. Very little money is needed to convert you from a bottle-by-bottle buyer to the proud possessor of a 'cellar'. Calculate what you spend on wine in three months, or two months, or at a pinch only one month – and spend it all at once in a planned spree. Put the wine away. Then continue to buy the same quantity as before but use it to replenish your stock, instead of for instant drinking. All you have done is to borrow three, two, or one month's wine money and the interest on that is your only extra expenditure. Your reward is wine you have chosen carefully and kept well, ready when you want it, not when you can get to the shops.

Make an effort to be clear-headed about what you really need. Do not spend more than you can comfortably afford. Think twice before buying unknown wines as part of a package. Do not buy a quantity of wine you have never tasted and might not like. Consider whether home delivery is really practicable: will there be someone at home to answer the door? Can you easily lift a full case of wine, especially a case that comes in a wooden box?

One of the wiliest ways of broadening your buying scope is to join with a small group of like-minded people to form a syndicate. A syndicate can save money by buying bigger lots of wine, thus bringing within reach extraordinary bottles at prices that would make you, on your own, feel guilty for months.

Make an effort to be clear-headed about what you really need.

Vintages

How come the clamour for famous vintages gets louder and louder as the differences between one year and another get smaller and smaller? Vintages are growing more consistent, with fewer duds. To most wine buyers the year is less important these days than the competence of the producer, and producers by and large are getting smarter every year.

Does this make you choke on your Pétrus, as *The Sunday Times* supposes? I put forward the proposition in the foreword to my *Pocket Wine Book* one year. Washout vintages have been rare recently; most produce fair-to-excellent wines, depending on the skill of the producer. We are dealing in nuances, not absolutes. But the small print of vintage quality and character, I said, the details of who picked before the rain, who avoided over-extraction in a hot year, is lost in the fanfare of another Year of the Century or the chorus of faint praise for a 'normal' vintage. Price and collectibility are based on the simplistic megaphone pronouncements that suit modern marketing. Not that this is particularly new: what is new is that better understanding of vine management and wine chemistry combine with higher profits and stricter selection to make truly poor wine unnecessary. Stick to a good producer and never mind the vintage – let alone spend a fortune on a famous one.

What is it about vintages? The word, unqualified, is used as a term of praise – presumably, for lack of a better explanation, because port only has a year attached if it is a good one. Non-

To most wine buyers the year is less important than the competence of the producer

vintage champagne is the run-of-the-mill stuff. When Bordeaux has tried in the past to sell a cross-vintage blend nobody has been interested. I am prepared to bet, notwithstanding, that most people think vintage variation is something they could do without.

To you and me it may be inherently interesting and enjoyable to distinguish between, let's say, a Bordeaux '95 and '96, or '04 and '06. It's fun to some to follow the flavour of late-ripening Cabernet or earlier-ripening Merlot as it shapes the character of a bottle. To some, but not to most. Simple certainties are what most wine-buyers want. How can it be bad news that progress makes it easier to find them?

Is climate change a contributing factor? Common sense tells us yes. Rising average temperatures are best news for marginal vineyards, furthest from the equator, where grapes ripen slowly to produce the most complex and longest-lasting flavours. German wine-growers, with a cooler climate than any, have already been in Nirvana for nearly 20 years. Australians are not so happy.

Judging wine

Why does a mother hold her child's nose when there is medicine to swallow? The nose is the aerial for the organs of taste in your tongue, palate and throat. Cut off the aerial and you don't get much of a picture. It makes bitter medicine tolerable. But it's a terrible waste of good wine.

Yet isn't this in effect what most wine drinkers do without thinking? Watch them. They give their glass a cursory glance (to make sure there's something in it), then it goes straight to their lips. The configuration of our faces obliges it to pass beneath the nose. But how often do you see it pause there, for the nostrils to register its message? Not often. The art of getting the most from wine is not complicated. But it does have to be learned.

Lesson one is to give it a chance. Any wine that is worth a premium is worth more than a clink and a swallow. How else do you justify the premium?

The art of tasting has been expounded and expanded to fill volumes. Professional tasters stake their names, and large sums, on subtle distinctions that give grounds for investing in a wine's development far into the future. They analyse its character, quality, chemistry, potential, and value like a jeweller assessing a stone. But we are talking about enjoyment, not analysis. We start, then, with a straightforward list of wine's distinctive characteristics and pleasures: the points not to be missed.

The art of getting the most from wine is not complicated. But it does have to be learned.

Judging wine: eye

The first is the colour, limpidity, viscosity, brilliance of the wine; its physical presence in the glass. It is the appreciation of the eye. A potent little pool of amber brandy, a glistening cherry tumbler of a young Italian red, the spring-leaf green that tints the pale gold of a glass of Chablis, a sleek ellipsoid of glowing ruby from Bordeaux or the crystal turbulence of Champagne all carry different messages of anticipation. Each is beautiful. Each means something. Each is worth appreciative inspection. Gradations of colour can tell a practised eye the approximate age of a wine – sometimes even its vintage and the variety of its grapes. Each

wine has an appropriate colour that experience can teach us to recognise. Cabernet-based wines, for example, are nearly always a deeper, darker red than Pinot Noirs. If the wine looks pale and thin the odds are that it will taste that way.

The wine's texture, or viscosity, can be equally revealing. Strong wines with concentrated flavours, like blood, are thicker than water. Where such wines wet the sides of the glass they tend to cling, then, as the alcohol evaporates, fall back in trailing drops that the Germans call 'church-windows'; the British 'legs', and the romantic, 'tears'.

Gradations of colour can tell a practised eye the approximate age of a wine – sometimes even its vintage and the variety of its grapes.

Step one in sizing up a wine is simply to look at its appearance in the glass. Hold it up against a white background such as a sheet of paper. Tilt the glass away from you so that you can see the colour, clarity, and depth of the wine at the rim. With practice this simple trick will enable you to tell a wine's approximate age.

Strong and sweet wines tend to stick to the glass, forming 'tears' or 'legs' as they fall back. The explanation is not as simple as it might seem: alcohol adheres to the glass better than water but evaporates more quickly. As it evaporates the wine's water content loses its adhesion and descends. Put your hand over the glass: evaporation stops and so do the 'tears'.

Judging wine: nose

When a professional, a winemaker or merchant, swirls the wine around in his glass before sniffing and sipping he is deliberately aerating the wine as forcefully as possible. Your nose can detect only volatile substances. Some wines are naturally highly aromatic, others less so. The less aromatic the wine is, the more a taster has to worry the scent out, sniffing for clues like a bloodhound.

The aromas of young wines are essentially the smell of the grapes, transmuted and intensified by fermentation. Unsurprisingly the grapes that make the easiest wines to identify (and at an elementary level, to enjoy) have the most distinctive and memorable smells (aromas is the accepted term) from the moment they become wine. Chardonnay, curiously enough, is not one of these aromatic grapes. It is the people's choice because it makes such a satisfying mouth- (rather than nose-) full – and because it is commonly seasoned with oak. If new wine is kept in oak barrels the scent of oak overlays and partially conceals the grape smell for a while. (A common short-cut is to add oak essence). After the wine is bottled and as it ages the components react and merge. Complex new aromatic substances form. With luck – but not with oak essence – a bouquet is born.

The aromas of young wines are essentially the smell of the grapes, transmuted and intensified by fermentation.

Judging wine: mouth

Nose and mouth are not separate organs of sensation. The blocked nose prevents the mouth from tasting. What the nose detects by sniffing, the mouth will confirm by sipping. But only the tongue and palate can reveal the sweetness, sourness or bitterness, the fruitiness, the acidity and the tannins, tough or tender, that in their various proportions and interactions make up the taste.

They certainly don't if the wine goes by the vodka route: straight from glass to stomach. Even if it interrupts the conversation, give your wine time to have its say. This means holding it in your mouth for a couple of seconds; for greater effect even chewing it ruminatively. And for maximum effect (but maybe not at dinner) pursing your lips and sucking a thin stream of air through it. The effect of this, while you hold a little wine between your lips and your tongue, is to turn up the volume on the flavour. You may well be surprised how much flavour a mouthful packs if you give it its chance.

Here is a bit of elementary analysis to help you focus on the flavour. Think of it in three stages. The first is the 'attack'. Is it agreeable or aggressive? The second is the 'middle palate' – does it expand on your tongue and satisfy every inquisitive taste-bud? And the third is the 'finish'. What flavour is there left after you have swallowed – and for how long? Poor wines leave either a nasty taste or none at all. Fine wines linger in departing sweetness. And great wines perfume the breath for a full five minutes, maybe more, after each sip.

You may well be surprised how much flavour a mouthful of wine packs if you give it its chance.

Assessing the first mouthful: taste is a combination of what the nostrils have already detected, plus the effect of the alcohol and the non-volatile elements – acids, sugars, tannins, and traces of minerals. A generous sip is needed to allow the wine to reach every part of the mouth. Only at this stage can you judge the full 'feel' of the wine.

'Chewing' the wine allows you to assess its 'body' – the sum of its flavours combined with the warmth and kick of its alcohol. Some tasters draw a little air between their lips and through the wine at this point to help maximise the impresssion. When you finally swallow, notice what flavour lingers on your palate and in the throat, and for how long.

Opening the bottle

It has taken centuries – over 60 of them – to develop the perfect container for wine. Now we have it, the greatest invention of the 17th century: the bottle and cork.

A wine bottle is not just a container. It is a sealed vessel in which the wine, protected from the air, holds its complex potencies in readiness for the day when it is drunk. Once the bottle is opened the wine is exposed to the destructive effects of oxygen. There is no going back.

Pulling a cork therefore always has a touch of drama about it; sometimes more than a touch when the cork is unwilling to yield to muscle and corkscrew.

To take an extreme case, here is what you do if the cork proves totally immovable. Take the heaviest kitchen knife you can find. Hold the bottle in one hand, with the neck pointing away from you, and the knife in the other, with the blunt edge toward the bottle. Now run the blade up the neck as hard has you can, hitting the 'collar' of the bottle with a terrific whack, and the neck should break off cleanly. Ridiculous? Strange to say it is almost routine in some of the more 'swagger' Champagne houses, where they use a sabre. (A hussar uniform helps, too.) But practise first. Your dinner guests will never forget it.

Pulling a cork always has a touch of drama about it.

Opening: corkscrews

I once forgot the corkscrew at an opera picnic and was obliged to do an impromptu survey of how the upper middle classes open their wine bottles. What I have to reveal is not pretty reading. I was left uncomprehending. The bottles on the tables were considerably in excess of the usual average 'spend' we are told about, but the corkscrews might as well have come out of crackers. Could this be why the screw cap is having an easy ride to the top?

The first corkscrew I tried came, I was told, from a supermarket. It was a weird hybrid lever device, heavy and silvery, with a screw so short that it only penetrated half the cork and pulled the top off. Did anyone have an old-fashioned long, straight, T-shaped corkscrew to rescue the situation? They did not. I had to push the cork in with a fork handle, always a sticky operation, and hold it down in the wine while I poured the first glass full of fragmented cork. I admit I forgot the cork when I tasted the wine; it was Chassagne Montrachet La Romanée 2004 from Vincent Girardin, a sumptuous success from a site high on the slopes towards Santenay. A good choice, I thought, for the opera that night: Donizetti's *L'Elisir d'Amore*.

But my corkscrew-scrounging foray had revealed horrors worse than the supermarket device. There was a twin-lever model pressed out of some depressing shiny substance with a

What stands between the affluent consumer and the elixir he is so eager for? His miserly attitude to the necessary utensil.

helix shape so that you can look up the centre. Nothing else grips cork well enough to guarantee it all comes out together.

You also need a waiter's friend, which is essentially a folding model of the above to go in your pocket. It has a flange to act as a purchase against the rim of the bottle and save back-bending effort.

gimlet for a screw, whose only result could be to pull the centre out of the cork. There were 'waiters' friends' so tiny and made of materials so thin and sharp that they cut your fingers. There were models built as robustly as a dry-cleaner's coat hanger and others of such chunky pretension that you looked for the book of instructions.

What is it that stands between the affluent consumer and the elixir he is so eager for? His miserly attitude to the necessary utensil. Here is what you need for easy access: a straight old-fashioned corkscrew, at least 100 mm long and at least 10 mm wide, made of forged metal, not bent wire, in a hollow

If you open a lot of bottles in short order the luxury you can easily afford (think one bottle of vintage champagne) is a lever pull, the one that looks like a crouching rabbit – perhaps not for the opera picnic, but for when the hordes descend to drink your cellar dry.

And screw caps ? I love them. They seem a bit humdrum for a costly bottle, and I hope somebody improves the aesthetics pretty soon, but for all wines (white, red, or rosé) I expect to open within a shortish period they are a very welcome development. What I can't stand are plastic corks; ugly and hard to pull. The smartest new closure is a glass and acrylic stopper; you are bound to see one soon.

Opening: corks that break or won't budge

Occasionally corks are too tight and break up (especially if the corkscrew you are using is badly designed). Or they may have grown crumbly with age and need kid-glove treatment. Then again, they may be too loose and get pushed in, at which point you are rewarded with a wine fountain and a sticky arm.

What if a cork comes to pieces? One technique worth trying, to remove a fragment out of reach in the neck, is to put the screw in again at the most oblique angle you have room for, then push toward the side of the neck at the same time as pulling upwards.

You squeeze the cork against the glass and hold it in one piece while gently pulling it out.

If that fails, and you are left with a cork in pieces in the neck and fragments floating in the wine, you might as well push the rest in. There is a fairly effective device made of three pieces of wire which will retrieve the bigger bits of cork easily enough from bottles with sloping shoulders. If it's a Bordeaux-type bottle with more pronounced shoulders, simply pour past them. You will get cork in your wine – at least in the first glass – but never mind; it won't affect the taste.

You will get cork in your wine but never mind; it won't affect the taste.

Opening: is it corked?

The two questions that crop up most frequently about opening a bottle of wine are when to open it, and how to tell if it is corked.

The first is easy to answer: it doesn't matter. Just pulling the cork makes no difference unless you decant the wine. There is simply not a big enough surface area of wine exposed to the air.

But corkiness will always be a worry – especially as these days it is happening more and more often. Some merchants put the figure of bottles more or less tainted by bad corks as high as 5 per cent – enough, if they were all returned, to remove their profits entirely.

There are degrees. A badly corked wine smells strongly, unpleasantly and unmistakably of mould. The mould is in the pores of the cork; unfortunately once the wine has picked up the smell nothing can be done. Experienced noses, though, wrinkle at much lesser degrees of the same smell, and convention allows them to return the bottle to the unfortunate supplier.

In my experience most people either don't recognise corkiness or are not offended by it enough to say anything. I have often found the taint in a wine being drunk more or less happily by half a dozen neighbours at a dinner. If I mention it (at low levels I grin and bear it) they often admit to being disappointed in the wine – but rarely know why.

I'm pretty sure that if I suggested we all went Swiss and did away with corks altogether the response would be horror. Wine is a marvellous amalgam of refreshment and romance, exoticism and relaxation. Nobody is obliged to play. But who wants to miss the fun?

Serving wine

In a logical no-nonsense world wine bottles would have screw caps like lemonade. And I suppose all their labels would be written in English too. But wine is a field where lack of logic is not just tolerated, it is the people's choice. Where is the sense in sticking corks in tens of millions of bottles of Beaujolais Nouveau for them all to be yanked out again within the month? The sense, of course, is in the symbolism. Corks are what makes wine different, its opening an act of celebration. Only the Swiss are grown-up enough to accept screw caps without question, even on their best bottles. The rest of us prefer the foreplay of cork and corkscrew, tug and pop.

Symbolism and ritual surround every stage of opening and serving wine. I've lost count of the times I've been asked why the port decanter has to go round the table clockwise. It doesn't matter whether you answer that it's because Nelson only had one arm, or that witches put a hex on anything that goes widdershins. The question,

like the port, still comes round again, because the probable true answer – that it doesn't matter a damn, so long as circulating decanters don't run into one another with sticky results – lacks the mystique that comes free with every bottle.

Thus there is a 'right', or at least conventional, way to handle every wine and every wine occasion, and you won't have failed to notice the growth of the sommelier industry to make sure the mysteries are marketed – I should say preserved and appreciated – properly. In my experience, though, serving wine is at the same time both simpler and more full of doubts and queries than the conventional wisdom would have us believe.

The absolute essentials are indeed minimal: a corkscrew, a glass, and the means to raise or lower the temperature of the bottle. No single thing makes as much difference to the enjoyment of wine as the right temperature. More of this later.

Serving wine: glasses

The genius of Riedel, the Austrian glass-makers and promoters, has produced a revolution in the world's concept of a good wine-glass. The company's big-bowled, long-stemmed, ultra-thin glasses now dominate the table-scape of every restaurant that wants to sell expensive wines.

Riedel's claims could hardly be more all-embracing. The manufacturer asserts that different grape varieties need different-shaped glasses to bring out their flavours – and purports to prove it in tasting-room conditions. It is a seductive idea for a rich wine buff who wants to impress his friends. But for people with normal priorities (and the usual limited cupboard space) there is a less pretentious and more economical alternative: the glass recommended by the International Standards Organisation (the ISO) for professional tasting. Many other glass designs now adopt its principles and approximate proportions.

The principle is simply stated: to capture all the aromas of the wine and funnel them straight to your nostrils. There is no need for a big glassful of air to do this. In fact a large volume of air dilutes the scent of the wine: you have to sniff harder.

One of the worst glasses for showing off wine is the one almost universally used by caterers: the Paris goblet. Since ISO-style glasses are now so widely and cheaply available, though, their clients might well start insisting on glasses worthy of their wine.

A good wine glass captures all the aromas of the wine and funnels them straight to your nostrils.

Riedel invented the notion that every wine needs a different glass. It doesn't of course; two or three will do. But they make a good case — and the glasses look extremely elegant.

Serving wine: temperature

Each wine you open has a different pleasure (or at least a different experience) to offer. How are you to know what preconditioning will show it in its best light? This is where you have to use your imagination. Just what is the chosen wine supposed to offer? Beaujolais and burgundy, for example, give quite different sorts of pleasure. The trick is to picture to yourself, if you can, the flavour and function of each wine in its context, then judge how best to make it fit the bill. In many cases this is as easy as sticking the bottle in the fridge an hour beforehand. This is the approach for young Champagnes and other sparkling wines, all cheap and medium-price whites and rosés, and for light red wines in hot weather.

With such wines the effect you are looking for is a cold mouthful first, aromatic impact second. The weather, the temperature of the room, and even the day outside should be your guide as to the just-right temperature. Extremely cold wine can be welcome in summer (when in any case it will warm up quickly in the glass).

In winter your body wants comfort more even than refreshment. (If you are merely thirsty, drink water: wine and thirst are bad partners.) The quickest way to bring a bottle from room temperature to refreshingly cool is to plunge it in icy water; ice cubes and water mixed. (Ice cubes alone are much less efficient.) If even the eight minutes it takes a bucket is too long, add a handful of salt.

The simple cold mouthful approach goes wrong, though, with the more serious class of white wines: richer wines with denser texture and concentration whose aromas are not so immediate. A luscious late-picked Riesling has its own statement to make that goes far beyond coldness. Finding exactly the right temperature for these fine wines is slightly trickier. 'Cellar temperature' is usually cited as the ideal: about 11°C (52°F) delivers the satisfying feeling that all the flavours and aromas are developing on your palate; nothing is hidden.

This mouth-cool temperature is my personal preference for a wider range of wines than convention suggests. I like to drink Beaujolais this way (rather than chilled like white wine) and think it brings out the zing in young claret. Sherry, Madeira and tawny port are all best at this temperature. So are Tokaji, Jurancon, *vins jaunes,* and the whole category of wines with added oomph, either from long aging or overripeness or both.

It is, strange to say, the high-priced, 'classic' mature red wines that pose most problems. There is a wider range of opinion on how and at what temperature to serve great Bordeaux and burgundy, when to open the bottle and whether to decant it, than about any other wines.

I have been criticised for serving red wines too cool by those who want the warming effect to start at the lips. And frequently they have been right, because in my old draughty country house in winter there is almost nowhere to lodge bottles snugly for a day or two before drinking. In proper modern dwellings you merely bring the bottle into your living quarters

a day or two before you need it. The problem that is more likely to arise is that you live at a temperature of at least 21°C (70°F) and your wine tastes more or less mulled. This is the effect of temperatures much over 18°C (65°F): they volatilise the alcohol before the aromatic components you want to smell. The wine seems disproportionately heady; its flavour thinned.

	F	C	
	68	20	
	66	19	
Room temperature	64	18	
	63	17	Best red wines especially Bordeaux
Red burgundy	61	16	
	59	15	Chianti, Zinfandel, Côtes du Rhône
Best white burgundy, port, madeira	57	14	
	55	13	Standard daily reds
	54	12	Lighter red wines e.g. Beaujolais
Ideal cellar Sherry	52	11	
Champagne, Most dry white wines, Fino sherry, Tokaji Aszú	50	10	Rosés, Lambrusco
	48	9	
	46	8	
Domestic fridge	45	7	
	43	6	Most sweet white wines, sparkling wines
	41	5	
	39	4	
	37	3	
	35	2	
	33	1	
	32	0	

Serving wine: decanting

Countless earnest tasting panels have tried to produce 'scientific' evidence that decanting helps, or harms, or has no effect at all on flavour. Let me put the case for decanting as succinctly as I can.

If a wine has sediment (all mature red wines do, or should) there is no other way of serving it without stirring it up. The wine cradles beloved of pretentious restaurants have exactly this effect: they guarantee that the second half of the bottle is cloudy. A cradle should only ever be used for uncorking a bottle before decanting it.

Does decanting release and maximise aromas or dissipate them? It is a matter of timing. It does release them, but if a wine is already mature, its scent accessible and obvious, there is a risk that it will be dispersed in the decanter. Such wines should therefore be decanted only shortly before serving.

Younger wines that have yet to exhale their full expression of grapes and soil and sun need decanting long enough beforehand to start the process. This can apply equally to any wine, red or white, that is still in the adolescent stage. On first opening the bottle you may wonder where the perfume is: after an hour in a decanter you can be almost overwhelmed by it.

When to decant

My rule of thumb is to decant red Bordeaux and other quality Cabernet/ Merlot wines, and also Hermitage/ Shiraz of top vintages, on an inverse time-scale in proportion to their age.

On first opening the bottle you may wonder where the perfume is: after an hour in the decanter you can be almost overwhelmed by it.

The older the wine the shorter the decanting time. There is no golden rule: experience is the only guide.

I would start at zero (just before serving) for a fully-mature wine, at say 20–25 years. Its unveiling will be rapid enough to observe in your glass. I would allow about half an hour in the decanter for a wine of 15–20 years, an hour for 10–15, two hours or so for 5–10 years and mabye four for a wine under five years, still inevitably tight and closed.

For red burgundy I would halve the decanting time. Pinot Noir is far more volatile and free with its perfume – freer in some cases than Chardonnay. Top white burgundies can develop their perfumes enormously in the glass, and therefore also in the decanter. As for vintage port, I shall always remember being given a mysteriously wonderful, rich, smooth vintage one Christmas by a friend. I was at a loss to guess its age. It was a '63, decanted on November 25th!

And how to

I always decant on the kitchen table, using a torch pointing upwards to help

me see what I'm – or rather the wine is – doing. There is no trick about it, except to get the light to shine through the neck and shoulder of the bottle. And once you have started to pour, to keep going – it must go in one smooth flow until you see the dark swirl of sediment reach the bottle neck. Then stop; the job is done.

Only vintage port presents a special problem: simply that the bottle is made of such dark glass that you need a very bright light to shine through it. My answer to this is to go very slowly, and when I even suspect the massive deposit (happily it hangs together) is nearing the brink to switch from the decanter to a jug alongside. I may get some more clear wine that way – or I may just get a jug of sludge.

Storing wine

Do you mean I can't open it now? That depends. Any wine that's worth a premium is worth storing, at least for a few months, and maybe for years. In simplest terms, the better the wine the more there is to gain from patience.

The thing to remember is that wine is alive. Being alive, it reacts to certain physical stimuli (such as violent movements and extreme heat and cold). It also passes at a faster or slower rate through the process of ageing. The mark of the best wine is that it has the longest life span – given that it is kept in suitable conditions.

Everyday wine, the bulk stuff, is blended to be at the best age for drinking (usually very young) when it is bottled. Good examples of everyday wine are robust enough to live on happily for, say, six months to a year.

In fact, really well-chosen everyday wines can show a distinct touch of class if they are given a chance by being carefully stored for a year or so.

Don't assume, though, that old jug is better than new jug. The opposite is more likely to be true. But if a jug red strikes you as being unusually tasty for the category where most reds are fairly thin, give a few bottles a chance. Instead of opening them in quick succession, drink them at intervals of a month or six weeks. You will soon be aware whether you are watching improvement or decline – and drink the rest or keep it accordingly.

I would hesitate to keep low-price whites on the same principle. Freshness (if they have it) is often their main virtue, so don't miss it. Buy them only as you drink them.

The better the wine the more there is to gain from patience.

At the premium level things are, or should be, different. Whenever you pay more for a distinct style, whether it is an *Appellation Contrôlée* or something from a highly regarded winery, you are paying for extra flavour, extra vitality, extra nuance.

In living wine these qualities are rarely predictable. For several months after bottling, fine wines are often in a sort of state of dumb shock. They seem to sulk. Open them then and you will be disappointed by the lack of fragrance and flavour. It is worth, therefore, keeping all newly made and bottled fine wines for at least two or three months before even sampling them. Shipping them a distance to your home can give them the sulks almost as much as the original bottling can. Mature wines don't need such a long recovery period as new ones, but try to give them a few weeks' rest at least.

The rewards for storing the grander grades of wine increase in direct proportion to their initial quality. First Growths are traded, as well as drunk, because they are known to have the potential to live, gradually improving, developing and finally (when rarity adds to their value) declining over a period that can last anything between ten and 100 years.

Storing wine: keeping a cellar

Though nothing can quite equal either the atmosphere or the efficacy of an ancient underground cellar, cool, dark, and tranquil, all beams and cobwebs, the word and the fact today are usually interpreted in terms of some cramped, often pretty makeshift, space above ground. What is important, and what still makes a hole in the ground the best of all places to store wine, is the unchanging conditions in a cellar: a cool, even temperature, dark, calm, and a certain degree of humidity. With ingenuity these conditions can be achieved in a cupboard under the stairs, in the back of a garage ... anywhere in fact that can be insulated. Most modern wine cellars are contrived in less-than-ideal conditions. But don't be put off. Given reasonable consideration most wines survive.

The first requirement is that the wines be kept at a reasonably even temperature, neither too warm nor too cold, but somewhat below normal room temperature. This means anything between 7–18°C (45–64°F). The ideal is about 10°C (50°F). At 10°C your white wines will be kept constantly at the right temperature for serving, and the red ones will mature slowly but steadily.

Slow and moderate fluctuations in temperature will not harm the wines,

Most modern wine cellars are contrived in less-than-ideal conditions. But don't be put off.

but sudden and violent changes will age them prematurely.

Darkness is important because light will age a wine before its time, especially if it is in a clear bottle – and ultraviolet rays will penetrate even dark-tinted glass. This is why you should never buy a fine wine off a brightly lit shelf in a store.

Moderate humidity keeps a cork in a good, pliable, resilient condition and stops it from shrinking. If your storage room is unduly dry you can install a humidifier or improvise one in the form of a bowl of moist sand.

Too much humidity will not damage the wine, but it soon rots cardboard boxes and encourages mould on labels. The label is the gauge of the value of a bottle; you can't afford to let it moulder. If this may be a problem there is a simple solution: before you store a bottle give the label a squirt with some scentless hair lacquer or artist's fixative. Either makes a reasonably permanent seal against damp.

The cellar should not suffer from the shakes. Calm repose without vibration is ideal for wine. In practice this is unlikely to be a problem in most homes. The small vibrations encountered in an average house do no harm.

Let us suppose that your dwelling, like most people's, is cellar-less (in the traditional sense). How do you set about creating the best storage conditions for your wine? Your first problem is likely to be space. If you live in your own house it is sometimes possible to have a small cellar dug out – say under the floor of your garage. A pre-cast concrete spiral cellar, ready to be sunk like a well under the floor, is an ingenious and excellent solution – if not a cheap one. Failing some such investment, you will have to make do with available space where conditions are approximately right. Ideally you should find a small room or cupboard without an outside wall and insulate it

generously. Limited in space, though. The bottom of a wardrobe might do at a pinch. A much better solution is a temperature-controlled storage unit: a kind of refrigerator about 4°C (39°F) warmer than the normal. EuroCave is a principal maker (the name has largely been adopted as the generic for such appliances). For those who have small apartments these are surely the best answer. A traditional wine merchant will usually store (for a small fee) wine until you have room for it. The step beyond (and may you reach it soon) is an insulated, air-conditioned room.

Storing wine:
how long must I keep it?

Although it is certainly true that far more good wines are drunk too early than too late, it is a bitter moment when you open a bottle and find it 'over the hill', faded, dried-out, or flattened by age. So how long should you keep it?

There never will be a cut-and-dried answer. The better sort of vintage chart tells you, in general terms, when each vintage of each important region is nearing maturity. But let us suppose you have had a bottle for three, or five, or ten years and you want to know whether there is any advantage in keeping it longer. Read the charts, read the wine magazines. But also look at the bottle.

Red wines reveal a lot about themselves by their colour, even through the glass of the bottle. Young wines are clearly red or purple, varying in intensity from vintage to vintage, region to region and grape variety to variety. If a red wine is impenetrably dark when held against a light bulb, the odds are that the flavour will be impenetrably intense, young and (maybe) harsh. Look at a few bottles against the light and you will quickly learn that young Bordeaux, for example, is usually much darker than young burgundy. Look at ten-year-old bottles of both and you will see how both have faded away from purple and toward red-brown. Prime time for good wines is usually when the wine is just moving across the spectrum of red into faint hints of brown or orange.

White wines move the other way – from very pale to straw to gold to amber. Only such noble sweet wines as Sauternes and Tokaji should ever be kept beyond the transition from straw to gold – which is easy to see through the (usually clear glass) Sauternes bottle. Respect a fine white wine's pedigree, and give it at least a year, preferably two or three – but then drink it. Only a great white burgundy or a Spätlese or Auslese from a top German grower calls for the ten-year treatment. But do believe what you read about the finest wines – red or white. It is a crying shame to drink them while they are still pubescent.

Storing wine:
stacks and racks

Old-fashioned cellars were designed with so-called 'bins' – simple shelves on which you piled the bottles as many as ten deep, because you bought your wine by the barrel and it was all the same. Even the label is a relatively new invention. A case of port delivered to my cellar back in 1965 had no labels. The shipper was identified only by the embossed end of the capsule. Each bottle just had a white paint mark to show which way up it should be. You can – indeed you should – use a label in the same way: keep the label uppermost and any sediment will be at the bottom when you come to pouring. You will also be able to read it easily.

The trouble with using the bin method today is that we don't buy vast quantities of one wine – indeed, few of us buy vast quantities at all. We may perhaps have only one bottle of a particular wine, and we need to be able to winkle out individual bottles easily. So we need racks.

A rack is simply a structure with a series of pigeon-holes, each hole capable of holding one or more bottles. Racks with one-bottle apertures are the most useful all-rounders. Another model is deep enough to allow two bottles to be placed end to end in each aperture. You can mislay bottles in the back of these and come across them as a pleasant surprise months (in my case sometimes years) later.

The commonest and best type of manufactured wine rack is made of wooden bars connected by galvanised metal strips in a modular system. There are any number of ways you can make your own bottle rack or improvise one. Short lengths of drainpipe are a practical and easy dodge. Wooden wine-cases are too good to throw away; they can be adapted. Even the ordinary cardboard boxes wine arrives in can make quite a serviceable temporary rack, provided of course that the room is dry.

Storing wine:
keeping track of your stock

It's a fair bet that once you have put a bottle away you will forget which slot you put it in. If you are to use your precious storage space with any efficiency at all a bit of book-keeping is essential. It needn't be difficult. Just mark each row and column of your wine rack with a number or letter (say, numbers horizontally, letters vertically). Each aperture will have, as it were, a grid reference consisting of a letter and a number. Whenever you store a bottle simply write this reference in your notebook (and cross it out when you drink the bottle). With such a system you can even scatter a dozen bottles of one wine all over the cellar, wherever there happens to be a vacant slot, and find them all again easily. Any other method wastes precious storage space.

White wines

Dry white wines

with a simple flavour and without very distinct aromas

Wines made from grapes with no readily identifiable aroma form the bulk of this category. Most are the equivalent of background music – agreeable, but not a concert performance demanding your attention. Youth and freshness are essential: these wines get tired quickly. They are often drunk as aperitifs, but can rapidly become boring without the addition of another flavour. Blackcurrant juice (cassis) is a favourite. With soda or sparkling mineral water they make a 'spritzer'. The wine trade looks disapproving, but I'm a great spritzer fan. As partners to food these wines have almost limitless uses, rarely rising to gastronomic heights but always helping the appetite along with fish, cold meats, garlicky dishes or curries which would smother fine wines. Serve them a few degrees colder than better or more delicate whites.

Most branded dry whites, jug or carafe wines fit into this category. They are usually made in large quantities in a warm climate – the San Joaquin Valley of California, for example. The leaders of this group, those with names and histories, include Muscadet, Entre-Deux-Mers and other simple white Bordeaux, supermarket-level Chablis, Gaillac, most Sylvaner and Pinot Blanc from Alsace, Aligoté from Burgundy and everyday Mâcon Blanc. Picpoul de Pinet from the Midi and Italy's everyday Soave, Frascati, Pinot Bianco, Pinot Grigio, Trebbiano, and Orvieto Secco usually belong in this category; Italian taste in white wines is traditionally neutral, as though the taste and smell of grapes gave offence. Austrian everyday white belongs here, as do the simpler offerings of much of Eastern Europe; California's and Australia's cheaper whites too. Most unoaked Spanish and Portuguese whites (though not Godello, Rueda or Vinho Verde) belong here. Switzerland's Fendant and Johannisberg can be remarkably potent and convincing examples.

Tasting Notes

Name of wine:

Producer: Year: Price:

Appearance:

Nose:

Palate:

Conclusions:

Food match:

Name of wine:

Producer: Year: Price:

Appearance:

Nose:

Palate:

Conclusions:

Food match:

As partners to food, dry white
wines have almost limitless uses,
always helping the appetite along
with dishes which would
smother fine wines.

Tasting Notes

Name of wine:

Producer: **Year:**   **Price:**

Appearance:

Nose:

Palate:

Conclusions:

Food match:

Name of wine:

Producer: **Year:**   **Price:**

Appearance:

Nose:

Palate:

Conclusions:

Food match:

Tasting Notes

Name of wine:

Producer: Year: Price:

Appearance:

Nose:

Palate:

Conclusions:

Food match:

Name of wine:

Producer: Year: Price:

Appearance:

Nose:

Palate:

Conclusions:

Food match:

Lightweight aromatic

whites with grapey flavours and more or less fruity/flowery scents

Germany provides the models for this category. The object is the scented crispness of fresh fruit, either balanced with a degree of sweetness or in the dry *Trocken* style that points the way forward, certainly for German drinkers.

German Riesling, sweet or dry, has a transparency, a tautness, that makes it one of the world's great wine styles; a Riesling from a great site on the Rhine or Mosel is the most exquisite of all wines for solo sipping. Use wines like these for wine parties and as aperitifs, drink them while reading or watching television – any time when refreshment and fragrance are more important than flavour and alcohol. In summer they are perfect garden wines, thoroughly chilled. In winter I like an after-dinner glass just pleasantly cool. The stepping stones from delicate to rich are Kabinett, Spätlese, Auslese. Ausleses were formerly all sweet; today they are frequently fully fermented to become dry – they are very potent but less original.

France's aromatic answers are Rieslings and Gewürztraminers from Alsace (which are weightier in body and alcohol and usually drier), Viogniers (richer and heavier) from the Rhône and the Midi, and Sauvignon Blancs from the Loire (Touraine), the Dordogne, parts of the south-west and even, these days, the Midi too.

Austrian Riesling can be also one of the most thrilling and convincing examples of this most appetising style of wine. The Italian Alto Adige and Friuli regions and adjacent Slovenia excel here as well, but Italy is also producing beautifully aromatic whites further south in Campania from the Fiano, Falanghina, and Greco di Tufo grapes, and in the Veneto from Garganega. Hungary has its Furmint and Hárslevelü grapes; Furmint has marvellous palate-cleaning acidity.

Australia offers its exceptionally tasty Rieslings with a characteristic petrol smell. In the USA, New York

Tasting Notes

Name of wine:

Producer: Year: Price:

Appearance:

Nose:

Palate:

Conclusions:

Food match:

Name of wine:

Producer: Year: Price:

Appearance:

Nose:

Palate:

Conclusions:

Food match:

state is making some very creditable Rieslings, and Virginia some remarkable Viogniers. New Zealand's Sauvignon Blancs are full of grassiness and passionfruit aromas, though its Rieslings have some way to go.

South Africa's Sauvignon Blancs are a halfway house between the New and Old Worlds, balanced and ripe. Argentina's Torrontes is outrageously perfumed; memorable, if hard to match with anything.

Tasting Notes

Name of wine:

Producer: Year: Price:

Appearance:

Nose:

Palate:

Conclusions:

Food match:

Name of wine:

Producer: Year: Price:

Appearance:

Nose:

Palate:

Conclusions:

Food match:

Assertive, full-bodied
dry whites with positive characters derived from the best grapes and/or maturity

White burgundy, the marriage of Chardonnay grapes and small oak barrels, is the epitome of this class. But all France's best dry whites have the same profile: relatively discreet aromas, mouth-filling flavour and firm structure, generous alcohol (about 13.5 degrees) giving appetising succulence without distinct sweetness. Their aim and purpose is to accompany food. They are fatiguing to drink without it. Their flavour is as strong as that of most red wines; don't lose it by over-chilling.

The list starts with the Chardonnay grape almost everywhere it is grown. It needs at least a year in bottle, usually two or more, to reach its full flavour. High-quality mature wines from the following grapes and areas can be bracketed here as the best meal-time whites, with almost any savoury food: Chardonnay, Riesling (Alsace, Austria, Rhine), Sauvignon Blanc (Graves, Pessac-Léognan), Pinot Gris (Alsace, Pacific Northwest), Chenin Blanc (Anjou, South Africa), Sémillon (Bordeaux, Australia), Marsanne and Roussanne (the Rhône and Midi, Australia), Malvasia (Italy, Croatia), Grechetto (Italy), Grüner Veltliner (Austria). Also the best white Riojas and classic examples of Frascati, Soave, Verdicchio, most whites from Collio, and so on. Montilla and Manzanilla from Andalucía can be included in this list, and so can the traditional characters of Austro-Hungary: Furmint, Szürkebaràt, Rotgipfler, Ruländer – if you can find them.

Tasting Notes

Name of wine:

Producer: Year: Price:

Appearance:

Nose:

Palate:

Conclusions:

Food match:

Name of wine:

Producer: Year: Price:

Appearance:

Nose:

Palate:

Conclusions:

Food match:

Tasting Notes

Name of wine:

Producer: Year: Price:

Appearance:

Nose:

Palate:

Conclusions:

Food match:

Name of wine:

Producer: Year: Price:

Appearance:

Nose:

Palate:

Conclusions:

Food match:

Sweet white wines

These, like sweet dishes, come at the end of most people's meal-plan. Not all, though; the Bordeaux idea of heaven is foie gras not to the sound of trumpets but to the sip of Sauternes – a sublime marriage of the sweetest wine with the richest food.

Oddly, where most wines taste best with food of comparable or not dissimilar flavour, sweet wines show to their best advantage with contrasting food, or no food at all. However good a Sauternes may be, it doesn't add much to a beautiful apple tart. But it illuminates a savoury foie gras and faces up to strong and salty cheeses as no red wine can.

Sauternes (and its colleague Barsac) is the champion of sweet table wines. The other runners are 'liquorous' (sticky and golden, about 14 per cent) wines from the neighbouring Bordeaux villages of Ste-Croix-du-Mont, Loupiac, and Cérons, Monbazillac from the Dordogne not far away, and *moelleux* Loire wines made in ideal autumns in Anjou (Bonnezeaux, Quarts de Chaume,

Coteaux du Layon) and Vouvray. Alsace makes outstandingly high-flavoured late-picked Rieslings and Gewürztraminers that can be used in the same way. So does Austria with its Ausbruch and Beerenauslese wines from the Burgenland, and likewise Hungary since the renaissance of its fabled Tokaji. New Zealand, Australia and California also make superb, intense sweet Rieslings, Semillons and Sauvignon Blancs, and Slovenia and Romania make some excellent examples, often from local grape varieties. Eiswein, made from grapes frozen on the vine, is a rarity in Germany, but almost commonplace (and incredibly sweet) in Canada. Sweet wines can also be made by drying grapes to concentrate their sugars, and then fermenting them: Italy's Vinsanto is the classic example.

All these are powerfully flavoured and all (except Tokaji) fairly high in alcohol. Tokaji Aszu (at about 11 per cent alcohol) is the daddy of them all; a magic mix of intensity, richness and such clear sharp focus that you can almost fool yourself it's not sweet at all.

In contrast the rare, very sweet wines of Germany, top Ausleses, Beerenausleses and Trockenbeerenausleses, are low in alcohol (the sweeter, the lower) and, like their drier counterparts, are unquestionably best sipped after or between meals.

Perhaps the most aromatic of all sweet wines are made of Muscat grapes, in all degrees of sweetness and strength ranging from an almost treacly character (as in the brown liqueur Muscats of north-east Victoria, Australia) to wines of great delicacy and lightness. The lower Rhône Valley and delta produce some admirable sweet-but-not-heavy Muscats, led by Beaumes-de-Venise and Frontignan. Roussillon and Rivesaltes in the extreme south of France make stronger sweet wines, as do the Greek islands of Samos and Santorini, and South Africa's Vin de Constance has been successfully reborn. Sicily, Portugal (Setúbal), and the Crimea all make delicious but difficult to find brown Muscats.

Sweet wines show to their best advantage with contrasting food, or no food at all.

Tasting Notes

Name of wine:

Producer: Year: Price:

Appearance:

Nose:

Palate:

Conclusions:

Food match:

Name of wine:

Producer: Year: Price:

Appearance:

Nose:

Palate:

Conclusions:

Food match:

Tasting Notes

Name of wine:

Producer: Year: Price:

Appearance:

Nose:

Palate:

Conclusions:

Food match:

Name of wine:

Producer: Year: Price:

Appearance:

Nose:

Palate:

Conclusions:

Food match:

Sparkling wines

Sparkling wines,
with Champagne as the boss

There is an enormous range of quality and style between a plain white wine with bubbles and the sinful opulence of the silkiest Champagne. The best non-Champagne sparkling wines come from California – where several Champagne firms have established cellars – and Australia and New Zealand in the New World, with European contenders including Italy's Franciacorta and Trentodoc, and recently, with great promise, England. Spain's Cava is far better made than in the past, is consistently fresh and can be delicious. From France, Burgundy's Crémant de Bourgogne and the Loire's Crémant de la Loire don't emulate Champagne, but do what good fresh, dry, fruity bubbles can do. Germany's Sekt often has more grape flavour than we are used to in fizz, but tastes perfect in context.

All use the Champagne method (now known as the classic method or *méthode traditionelle*, thanks to the Champenois lawyers). Other sparkling wines, even Russian Champanski, can be fun, but are usually more so flavoured with fresh orange juice or a drop of syrup (blackcurrant, grenadine or strawberry). Italian Prosecco is attractive on its own and makes a feature of its mild softness and its lack of distinctive flavour; you soon forget how many glasses you've had. The ultimate 'fun' wines are sparkling Muscats, of very low alcoholic strength but honey sweetness, with Asti the one to choose.

Tasting Notes

Name of wine:

Producer: Year: Price:

Appearance:

Nose:

Palate:

Conclusions:

Food match:

Name of wine:

Producer: Year: Price:

Appearance:

Nose:

Palate:

Conclusions:

Food match:

Tasting Notes

Name of wine:

Producer: Year: Price:

Appearance:

Nose:

Palate:

Conclusions:

Food match:

Name of wine:

Producer: Year: Price:

Appearance:

Nose:

Palate:

Conclusions:

Food match:

Age, far from wearying good Champagne, adds dimensions and flavours you could never surmise from raw young fizz

Tasting Notes

Name of wine:

Producer: Year: Price:

Appearance:

Nose:

Palate:

Conclusions:

Food match:

Name of wine:

Producer: Year: Price:

Appearance:

Nose:

Palate:

Conclusions:

Food match:

Rosé wines

Rosé wines
from camisole pink to onion-skin orange

There is no prestige in being a middle-of-the-roader, but you collect a lot of friends. Everyone loves pink wines now; and everyone, but everyone, is making them. Every country that makes wine is making pink of some sort. Don't be too snobbish to try them.

Pink wines get their colour from the skins of red grapes, the wine being run off the skins once it has the right colour, but before it is toughened by the red-grape tannins. Any red grape can be used for rosé in this way, and in some part of the world most are: Pinot Noir, Cabernet Sauvignon, Cabernet Franc, Syrah/Shiraz, Carmenère, Grenache, Carignan, Tempranillo, Zinfandel ... Even Pinot Grigio appears in a pink version, with a (perfectly legal) admixture of up to 15 per cent of unnamed red grapes.

Some rosés have intrinsically more colour than others, and some regions tradionally prefer darker or paler shades of rosé. Provence rosé is very pale, Navarra rosado rather darker, most South American rosés darker again. Rosés can also be bone dry or somewhat sweeter; sweeter rosés, if from a warm climate where acidity is low, can be distinctly jammy to the taste. I can't imagine lunch in the South of France without my beaded bottle of rosé – to which I often add a splash of water.

Sparkling wines are in on the act, as well. Pink Champagne is one of the prettiest and most luxurious (that is, expensive) of all wines, and many of Champagne's imitators also make pink versions.

Tasting Notes

Name of wine:

Producer: Year: Price:

Appearance:

Nose:

Palate:

Conclusions:

Food match:

Name of wine:

Producer: Year: Price:

Appearance:

Nose:

Palate:

Conclusions:

Food match:

Tasting Notes

Name of wine:

Producer: Year: Price:

Appearance:

Nose:

Palate:

Conclusions:

Food match:

Name of wine:

Producer: Year: Price:

Appearance:

Nose:

Palate:

Conclusions:

Food match:

Red wines

Fresh grapey
young reds

This is a class of wine whose star seems, sadly, to be waning. The fashion for reds recently (though there are signs of a welcome change) has been bigger, richer, more concentrated: perhaps it's not surprising that rosé has risen so much in popularity. Some of the darkest rosés are effectively light reds.

The ideal light red wine crosses the (anyway vague) border into a class of flavour associated with white wine. Like whites they rely on acidity for their bite and liveliness (reds have acidity too, but back it up with tannin). In the conventional ordering of several wines, red comes after white. You can treat these wines as young whites – and serve them almost as cool. Above all don't try to age them: the bottom falls out. Without their simple childlike vitality they become dull and thin. Drink them young, with food (any food except highly savoury gamey dishes) or without. They go as well as white wine (and often better than mature red) with cheese.

Any wine sold as 'Nouveau', 'Primeur', 'Joven' or 'Novello' should be in this style: such wines have no oak ageing. Look for the most recent vintage. Beaujolais is the epitome of this style, though Beaujolais Nouveau never matches a properly made Beaujolais-Villages from a good producer, or a light cru like Fleurie or Chiroubles. Sometimes you can find simple young red Bordeaux like this; unoaked young Midi or Rhône wine is a good bet, too. The lively young Cabernet reds of Anjou and Touraine are often of this character, growing more serious only in warm vintages. Italy offers simple Valpolicella, Bardolino, and Chiaretto in this style, and sometimes a vivid Dolcetto from Piedmont, too. Lambrusco, traditionally at least, is this kind of wine with more bubbles; Rioja Joven from Spain, or much simple Tempranillo or Garnacha from across the country, is also appealingly light and fresh. Oddly I have never found a good example from the hot regions of the New World.

*Wine is like Cleopatra; infinite
in its variety.*

Tasting Notes

Name of wine:

Producer: Year: Price:

Appearance:

Nose:

Palate:

Conclusions:

Food match:

Name of wine:

Producer: Year: Price:

Appearance:

Nose:

Palate:

Conclusions:

Food match:

Tasting Notes

Name of wine:

Producer: Year: Price:

Appearance:

Nose:

Palate:

Conclusions:

Food match:

Name of wine:

Producer: Year: Price:

Appearance:

Nose:

Palate:

Conclusions:

Food match:

Standard low-price
reds, whether sold in jug, bag or bottle

This was once the most popular of all classes of wine, as France's *vin ordinaire*, blended to be just sufficiently tasty, reasonably smooth, moderately alcoholic, and a decent shade of red. Now it is no more: brands have taken over.

Some brands are international; some much smaller. The definition of a brand is a question too complicated to go into here: a marketing person would argue that Château Lafite is a brand, but it's not the sort of brand we're talking about. The brands I mean taste the same year in, year out, are blended to a bland acceptability with whatever characteristics the market demands, and are frequently discounted. Don't be fooled by such discounts. A wine that is notionally sold for £10, but discounted to £5, is not a bargain. The lower price was planned when the wine was made. If it tastes gloopy but thin, that's why.

This is not to say that brands are always poor value: some are perfectly respectable wines. But what they lack is individuality and personality. They have introduced many a beginner to wine and, providing you don't expect too much, they won't disappoint.

For refreshment's sake these wines are drunk on the cool side.

Tasting Notes

Name of wine:

Producer: Year: Price:

Appearance:

Nose:

Palate:

Conclusions:

Food match:

Name of wine:

Producer: Year: Price:

Appearance:

Nose:

Palate:

Conclusions:

Food match:

Tasting Notes

Name of wine:

Producer: Year: Price:

Appearance:

Nose:

Palate:

Conclusions:

Food match:

Name of wine:

Producer: Year: Price:

Appearance:

Nose:

Palate:

Conclusions:

Food match:

Medium to full-bodied
reds made for maturing

A pretty dull definition of the majority of the greatest red wines: red Bordeaux and burgundy, Rhônes and Riojas, the finest Cabernets, Pinot Noirs and Zinfandels of California, their equivalents from the Pacific Northwest and Australia, top Chianti Classicos and such originals as Sassicaia and Tignanello, Torgiano and Carmignano. Portugal enters its best garrafeiras from Dão, Douro, the Alentejo and Bairrada, Spain the cream of Penedès, Duero and Navarra reds, Chile, South Africa and New Zealand their fast-improving Cabernets and Merlots. Their common characteristic (though less so with the majority of New World wines) is that they need time, in barrel and bottle, to fulfil their potential. To drink a fine Bordeaux or burgundy before it is at least five years old is to forgo the quality you paid a premium for. Long vatting plumps them up with tannins, pigments, and all manner of tasty stuff. Time moulds these elements into what has been called 'a chemical symphony'. Harmony between the component flavours is what you are waiting for. The dark deposit you often find in wines of this class is the fall-out from these changes.

Don't overwhelm their flavours with the strongest-tasting dishes. Roast meats are excellent, poultry, too, but not well-hung game or any highly seasoned food. Beware also of cheese. Only the milder cheeses consort well with fine mature red wines.

Full-bodied reds need time, in barrel and bottle, to fulfil their potential.

Tasting Notes

Name of wine:

Producer: **Year:**   **Price:**

Appearance:

Nose:

Palate:

Conclusions:

Food match:

Name of wine:

Producer: **Year:**   **Price:**

Appearance:

Nose:

Palate:

Conclusions:

Food match:

To drink a fine Bordeaux or
burgundy before it is at least five
years old is to forgo the quality
you paid a premium for

Tasting Notes

Name of wine:

Producer: **Year:**   **Price:**

Appearance:

Nose:

Palate:

Conclusions:

Food match:

Name of wine:

Producer: **Year:**   **Price:**

Appearance:

Nose:

Palate:

Conclusions:

Food match:

The darkest, most
full-blooded, turbo-powered reds

Mediterranean regions, given the chance, will ripen red grapes to sticky blackness almost every year. In northern Europe it takes an exceptional summer. The result, in either case, is a darker, more potent wine than the normal Bordeaux or burgundy. California's Napa Valley made its name with this type of full-blooded wine. Most of the growers are now aiming for something more subtle. Châteauneuf-du-Pape and Hermitage, Bandol, Barolo, Barbaresco, Brunello di Montalcino, Vega Sicilia in Spain, Australia's massively succulent Barossa Shiraz are classics of the genre.

The rare vintages of Bordeaux that reach this degree of concentration have included 1945, '61, '82 and '90. Burgundy scarcely ever makes this kind of wine.

Black and daunting as these full-blooded red wines may be, they can be a memorable experience drunk young: tannic and sweet with concentrated fruit at the same time. In youth these wines can even match powerful cheeses. But when mature, with their colour ebbing and an autumnal smell coming on, they enter another realm of voluptuous sensations.

Black and daunting as these wines may be they can be a memorable experience drunk young.

Tasting Notes

Name of wine:

Producer: Year: Price:

Appearance:

Nose:

Palate:

Conclusions:

Food match:

Name of wine:

Producer: Year: Price:

Appearance:

Nose:

Palate:

Conclusions:

Food match:

Red wine is always the centrepiece of a dinner party, but alone at home it makes the perfect contemplative sipping, with a book by the fireside.

Tasting Notes

Name of wine:

Producer: Year: Price:

Appearance:

Nose:

Palate:

Conclusions:

Food match:

Name of wine:

Producer: Year: Price:

Appearance:

Nose:

Palate:

Conclusions:

Food match:

Tasting Notes

Name of wine:

Producer: **Year:**   **Price:**

Appearance:

Nose:

Palate:

Conclusions:

Food match:

Name of wine:

Producer: **Year:**   **Price:**

Appearance:

Nose:

Palate:

Conclusions:

Food match:

Fortified wines

Wines with added alcohol

'Fortified' or 'dessert' wines – port, sherry, Madeira and their look-alikes – have only one thing in common: they have been topped up with alcohol (brandy or another spirit) to make them stronger. Port is brandied to keep it sweet, sherry to keep it stable.

In Victorian times port and sherry (they were great rivals) accounted for about half of all the wine drunk in Northern Europe. They reached as high a degree of perfection as any wines – though of course there were always down-market brands. Fashion these days (or some say it's our central heating) has decimated their market. What's left, though, is the pick of the best for us to enjoy. Today's top ports and sherries are the best they have ever been. Fino sherry competes with champagne as the ultimate aperitif, and vintage port has no peer as the ultimate after dinner comforter.

Fortified wines can improve with age for improbable periods.

Tasting Notes

Name of wine:

Producer: **Year:**   **Price:**

Appearance:

Nose:

Palate:

Conclusions:

Food match:

Name of wine:

Producer: **Year:**   **Price:**

Appearance:

Nose:

Palate:

Conclusions:

Food match:

PINTA
2003
PRODUCED AND BOTTLED BY:
WINE & SOUL, LDA
AVENIDA JÚLIO DE FREITAS, VALE DE MENDIZ 5085-101, PINHÃO
20% alc. vol.
PRODUCE OF PORTUGAL

Tasting Notes

Name of wine:

Producer: **Year:**   **Price:**

Appearance:

Nose:

Palate:

Conclusions:

Food match:

Name of wine:

Producer: **Year:**   **Price:**

Appearance:

Nose:

Palate:

Conclusions:

Food match:

Favourite aperitifs

Sherry

The London *Evening Standard* reported in 2006 that sales of dry sherry in the UK rose 15 per cent in the previous year, something they have not done for a long time. But among drinkers aged between 35 and 45, they rose 81 per cent. A straw in the wind? A statistical blip? Who knows. But if I were a Champagne shipper I should see it as an ill omen. There is one wine, and only one, which can challenge the aperitif qualities of Champagne. Once the word gets round, Champagne's most powerful sales point, the bubbly assumption, loses its potency.

The bubbly assumption? The waiter springs to your table, menu in hand. 'What about something to start with, sir? A glass of Champagne?' You want to start on the right foot; you don't feel like Sauvignon Blanc, or want to quiz him about wines-by-the-glass. You know the mercurial effect of those bubbles in your blood stream. The easy answer is yes.

It's a long time since I was in the 35–45 bracket, but I have been asking for fino recently, too. I need a conditioner as much as anyone when I sit down to read a menu. But the rush of bubbles no longer seems the inevitable choice. The extra weight of a fino or manzanilla, its slight warmth in the mouth, its salty freshness, its hint of nuts, its suggestion of olives, is the savoury alternative. Sherry is unchallenging; it is no more

There is only one wine which can challenge the aperitif qualities of Champagne.

Tasting Notes

Name of wine:

Producer: **Year:** **Price:**

Appearance:

Nose:

Palate:

Conclusions:

Food match:

Name of wine:

Producer: **Year:** **Price:**

Appearance:

Nose:

Palate:

Conclusions:

Food match:

intellectual than Champagne, but a natural slow-sipper with enough in each sip to make you pause, reach for the bread basket, feel your appetite become palpable.

Champagne and sherry, I have always thought, are two sides of the same coin. Both are dry white wines from ideal (and almost identical) chalk soils, but with a climate problem. Straight up, unaided by art, they fail to make the grade. Champagne is too acid; sherry not acid enough. Enter an industry, in each case, to polish a rough diamond, to rebalance a clumsy wine and bring out its lustre. Centuries of experience later, after heaven knows what investment, the thing is as perfect as it can be, and not only perfect in its way but consistent, bottle after bottle, year after year.

Sherry, of course, is a fraction of the price of Champagne. To snobs this is its disadvantage: it has no bling factor. The rest of us may be happy to put the difference towards a better bottle to follow. Why not, though, keep going with another glass or two? For smoked salmon, soup, oysters, terrines or anything resembling tapas it is a perfect partner. Is this why restaurants are reluctant to serve sherry by the bottle? At per-glass prices it is already a bargain. At per-bottle it is a simple steal. Start now, before they figure out how to do a Krug.

Tasting Notes

Name of wine:

Producer: Year: Price:

Appearance:

Nose:

Palate:

Conclusions:

Food match:

Name of wine:

Producer: Year: Price:

Appearance:

Nose:

Palate:

Conclusions:

Food match:

Tasting Notes

Name of wine:

Producer: Year: Price:

Appearance:

Nose:

Palate:

Conclusions:

Food match:

Name of wine:

Producer: Year: Price:

Appearance:

Nose:

Palate:

Conclusions:

Food match:

Champagne and sherry, I have
always thought, are two sides
of the same coin.

Tasting Notes

Name of wine:

Producer: Year: Price:

Appearance:

Nose:

Palate:

Conclusions:

Food match:

Name of wine:

Producer: Year: Price:

Appearance:

Nose:

Palate:

Conclusions:

Food match:

Wine with food

Wine with food

Putting wine and food together in the ideal combination is a challenging and often controversial business. White with fish, red with meat is not a law, like driving on the left when you land at Dover. You are not going to hit anyone coming the other way. But you have to start somewhere.

I have always been guilty of choosing wines for people rather than for dishes. When on my own I drink what I feel like drinking. No, it isn't always Champagne. When it's a twosome, I find out (if I don't know already) what sort of wine my friend enjoys and open a bottle. When it's a larger party, a combination of the company, occasion, mood and domestic economy usually narrows the field enough to make choosing fairly easy. Occasion? Is it a family meal, a business lunch or an evening celebration? Mood? Do I feel lavish, experimental, or do I want to play it safe? Economy? I feel happier ordering something I can easily afford (especially in restaurants) than going for a mortgage, so to speak.

My attitude to wine comes with seeing it as a social drink rather than a condiment for food. Committed foodies may be scandalised, but I find the times are rare when my choice of wine is guided – rather than simply influenced – by the precise flavours of a dish.

I have always been guilty of choosing wines for people rather than for dishes.

Tasting Notes

Name of wine:

Producer: Year: Price:

Appearance:

Nose:

Palate:

Conclusions:

Food match:

Name of wine:

Producer: Year: Price:

Appearance:

Nose:

Palate:

Conclusions:

Food match:

Wine with food:
the art of matchmaking

An impressionistic approach gets you close enough. You have learned by experience what flavour to expect in, say, lamb or liver. With experience you learn approximately what weight and aroma to expect from, say, a fresh Beaujolais, a five-year-old Pomerol or a two-year-old Sonoma Chardonnay.

The art of matching wine with food consists of a moment's imagination – a mental scanning of the two repertoires. Think of them, if you like, as two colour wheels. You can turn them until you find a close match, or a total contrast, or some pleasing combination in between. The catch is that you need enough experience of different wines to colour your own wheel. Few people ever seem to get this far (and winemakers almost never: in Burgundy all they know is what food tastes good with burgundy).

The categories of wine outlined earlier are a start, at least, at devising a wine-wheel. It would be foolhardy to be categorical in the same way about food. Rather than make a long mouth-watering list of every dish, bland or spicy, let us see what we mean by contrasting flavours, and what matching them involves. Contrast (or complement) is epitomised by the

The art of matching wine with food consists of a moment's imagination – a mental scanning of the two repertoires.

Tasting Notes

Name of wine:

Producer: Year: Price:

Appearance:

Nose:

Palate:

Conclusions:

Food match:

Name of wine:

Producer: Year: Price:

Appearance:

Nose:

Palate:

Conclusions:

Food match:

appalling British habit of dousing fatty food with vinegary sauces. French-fried potatoes with tomato ketchup and jellied eels with vinegar like battery acid are a couple of gross examples. A rather more delicate one is Chablis with shellfish. Crab and lobster meat is rich, dense, and quite detectably sweet. The clean, slightly tart, mineral flavour of Chablis whets the appetite for more. A quite different sort of contrast between food and wine is found in the German taste for pairing pungent, well-hung game, venison or wild boar, with a sweet and velvety Riesling Auslese.

Sancerre on the Loire is known for two famous products: its aromatic dry white wine and its salty, crumbly, powerfully goaty cheese. The two are admirably complementary. Sancerre may be a light wine compared with, say, a red burgundy or a red Rhône, but its acidity and aromas fight back at the cheese in an ideal pairing, where a fleshy red wine would be helplessly pinned to the ropes. The extreme saltiness of real French Roquefort is already in contrast with its luxurious buttery texture. Add the sweetness of Sauternes to the richness of the cream and its bite is diminished to agreeable piquancy. The English follow the same principle in drinking fruity port with their highly savoury Stilton.

Closely paired flavours are commoner in practice than complementary ones. Take a couple of examples much favoured in Bordeaux: fragrant flesh of lamb from the riverside marshes with an almost herbal Médoc, or the fat lampreys of the Dordogne stewed in strong St-Emilion and served with the same wine on the table. Here the citizens of Bordeaux are matching food and wine in close harmony. Their apparently eccentric choice of Sauternes with dangerously rich foie gras follows the same logic. Even their habit of pouring old claret over wild strawberries, in place of cream, is designed to bring out a hint of strawberry in the wine, and no doubt vice versa – you have to taste this combination to believe it.

Tasting Notes

Name of wine:

Producer: **Year:**   **Price:**

Appearance:

Nose:

Palate:

Conclusions:

Food match:

Name of wine:

Producer: **Year:**   **Price:**

Appearance:

Nose:

Palate:

Conclusions:

Food match:

The clean, slightly tart, mineral
flavour of Chablis whets the
appetite for more.

Tasting Notes

Name of wine:

Producer: Year: Price:

Appearance:

Nose:

Palate:

Conclusions:

Food match:

Name of wine:

Producer: Year: Price:

Appearance:

Nose:

Palate:

Conclusions:

Food match:

Wine with food: problem pairings

There is a handful of flavours that never seem to work with wine. Oily smoked fish, such as smoked salmon, is difficult to match, but try fino sherry with it. There is a salty authority in the wine that emphasises the rich flavour of the salmon. Asparagus is not easy either; Sauvignon Blancs seem to echo the flavour, fat Chardonnays meet it head on; curiously enough such sweet wines as late-harvest Alsace give it zest.

Chocolate is the most notorious: neither pairing nor contrasting really seems to work. The most successful wines, for a reason I don't fully understand, seem to be Madeira and Tokaji. What they have in common is sweetness with a high level of acidity. Citrus fruit is very tricky. You can drink sweet wines with, say, caramelised oranges, but the wine almost disappears.

Sweet dishes in general tend to come off better than any sweet wines chosen to partner them. To me Tokaji works best of all – but when I say that it is only right that I declare a business interest (I helped to found a company to resurrect Tokaji after the calamities of communism). To taste port or Madeira or old Sauternes at their best try the contrast of a plain sponge cake, or a plate of filberts.

In the same way there are whole cultures of cookery that are, at least on the face of it, inimical to wine. Oriental food, whether Indian, Chinese, Japanese or any other, relies on seasonings that threaten to smother the taste of wine. Chilli fights with tannin; wasabi fights with everything. Ginger can be a problem, too. So choose the softest possible tannins in red wines, and if possible pull back on the chilli in the food. A touch of sweetness in the wine can help balance heat, as well. Riesling, Pinot Gris and Chenin Blanc are all sound choices with Chinese food, even Szechuan if it's not too hot. Try Chardonnay (this includes blanc de blanc Champagne) with good acidity

with tempura, dry sherry (whether fino or oloroso) with sushi, red burgundy with shabu shabu. New Zealand Sauvignon Blanc matches the lemon grass in Thai cooking. And very good, weighty, vintage Champagne can handle stronger flavours than you'd think, even Thai.

Just as food can smother the flavour of wine, so can another wine that is more full-bodied or flavoursome. Tradition has handed down to us a commonsensical order of play in which light wines come before weightier ones. This is often interpreted to mean that all (dry) whites should precede all red. But there are light reds and weighty whites. Let the volume of flavour, not the colour, be the guide.

Convention also decrees that in a meal with two similar wines – say two red Bordeaux of about the same quality but different ages – the younger should be served before the older. This is despite the fact that the older may be more faded and, in reality, lighter. There is good sense in the tradition: the more complex flavours of the older wine can make the younger taste simplistic and two-dimensional if it is served after. On the other hand I would serve a very old wine before a strong, strapping new one.

In practice I often prefer to serve the two similar wines side by side, or in quite rapid succession, so that friends can enjoy comparing and contrasting.

Experiment leads to unexpected harmonies; keep an open mind.

Tasting Notes

Name of wine:

Producer: Year: Price:

Appearance:

Nose:

Palate:

Conclusions:

Food match:

Name of wine:

Producer: Year: Price:

Appearance:

Nose:

Palate:

Conclusions:

Food match:

I often serve similar wines side by side, so that friends can enjoy comparing and contrasting.

Tasting Notes

Name of wine:

Producer: **Year:**   **Price:**

Appearance:

Nose:

Palate:

Conclusions:

Food match:

Name of wine:

Producer: **Year:**   **Price:**

Appearance:

Nose:

Palate:

Conclusions:

Food match:

Special occasions

Special occasions:
a little goes a long way

Logic tells you that the better a wine is the more of it you will want to drink. Indeed my own wine-judging system is based purely on desirability. The lowest possible score is one sniff: 'No thank you'. One sip is almost as dismissive, two faintly exploratory; one glass pretty damning, two either curious or desperate .... It becomes more telling when we reach the bottle level. If you want a second bottle it says something pretty positive about the first.

Yet doing the sums as a host preparing a party I find that if you give guests wine with the sort of concentrated character they can't miss, they will actually swallow less of it. In terms of flavour per unit of volume, great wine beats ordinary wine by a factor of, I would say, about ten to one – both in the strength of the flavour and, even more importantly, in its length in your mouth. This means each sip need be only one-tenth the size to make the same impression. Allow for the fact that the impression is delicious, and you want, shall we say, five times as

much of it, you still need only half as much volume. Translated into bottles, this means that one bottle of truly fine wine will go as far as two of plonk. No wonder they sell it in gallon jugs.

The French have a measure for the all-important factor of length of flavour – the time the taste persists after you have swallowed the wine. They call it a *caudalie*. One *caudalie* (from the Latin *cauda*, meaning a tail) equals one full second of lingering flavour. A plain Bordeaux rouge clocks up between one and two seconds before its taste disappears, while a (mature) First Growth perfumes your breath for ten, 12, even 20 or more seconds.

How, then, do you calculate how much wine you are going to need for a given occasion? A rough rule of thumb is that you need an average of one and a half glasses of an aperitif per person, followed by two glasses of wine with a meal, and possibly one more after the meal. A 75-centilitre (24fl oz) wine bottle gives six four-ounce portions. If

the aperitif, the table wine and after-dinner wine are all of 'normal' strength the total consumption is, therefore, four and a half glasses or three-quarters of a bottle a head.

If you serve two or three different wines with the meal, guests will probably drink an extra glass, bringing their total consumption up to nearly a bottle. Spread over an evening this is not excessive. Since an average person metabolises about one 'unit' of alcohol per hour, in theory this means that six units spread over three hours leaves you with only three units in your system. It is still not a subject I am anxious to discuss with a magistrate.

There is another phenomenon to be observed: the more people there are in a party the more each person is likely to drink. When you are on your own half a bottle seems enough wine, but when there are two of you one bottle scarcely seems enough. Two bottles can seem meagre for three people – they often feel like a third. Often four people need three, and can run to four. I suppose that the difference is accounted for by the energy you expend in conversation – that, and the time you spend over the meal.

Catering for a bigger party I usually assume that guests will somehow consume approximately one bottle of wine per head in total. This doesn't mean that I open that many bottles. I just make sure they're there.

And if wine is the main event, not supporting a meal but starring at a party with only canapés, what then? For a start, choose a wine of moderate flavour and strength. Rosé will please most people, but choose one which has acidity and freshness, and isn't jammy. Paler rosés are usually a safe bet, and look light and refreshing, which is also important. Rosé is particularly good in the summer, but is a year-round choice now as well.

Tasting Notes

Name of wine:

Producer: Year: Price:

Appearance:

Nose:

Palate:

Conclusions:

Food match:

Name of wine:

Producer: Year: Price:

Appearance:

Nose:

Palate:

Conclusions:

Food match:

Special occasions: white wine for parties

Choose a wine with a definite style but not too much assertiveness. Wine drunk alone should not shout. Light Austrian Grüner Veltliner is ideal: structured but subtle. Or try Italy, especially the Alto Adige, or one of the numerous non-aromatic but nicely crisp whites of the Soave-Frascati-Orvieto-Verdicchio-Vermentino-Gavi gang. Pinot Grigio is usually innocuous, Garganega more aromatic and interesting; both should go down well. Likewise the fairly substantial dry whites of Friuli. There are lots of good whites from the south, too, including quite aromatic grapes like Fiano, Falanghina and Greco di Tufo. Slovenia and Croatia are also good sources for well-made, subtle whites. Good German wine is always a hit, even among those who think they don't like German wine; they're living in the bad old days of Liebfraumilch. Give them a good Riesling, don't tell them what it is, and they'll love it.

Lighter, crisper whites are being made everywhere now. Australian Riesling has great crispness and purity, but New Zealand Sauvignon Blanc can be a bit too aggressive. If you want Sauvignon, try South Africa, from somewhere cool like Elgin. Among French wines I would choose simple light dry white Bordeaux, Alsace Pinot Blanc or dry Muscat, or a Sauvignon Blanc from the Loire. I would tend away from Chablis or Mâcon Blanc which can become tiring to drink without food. And it's worth looking again at Portugal's Vinho Verde: wines based on the excellent Alvarinho or Loureiro grapes have lovely aroma and plenty of fresh acidity.

I would not recommend US jug wines, except perhaps as a 'spritzer' or the base of a fruit cup. New York state Riesling has the right sort of freshness, but California wines, and even those from Washington or Oregon, can be over-weighty for party drinking – at least to my taste. These wines are not on the whole as thirst-quenching as wines from Europe: an essential quality in a good party wine.

Tasting Notes

Name of wine:

Producer: Year: Price:

Appearance:

Nose:

Palate:

Conclusions:

Food match:

Name of wine:

Producer: Year: Price:

Appearance:

Nose:

Palate:

Conclusions:

Food match:

Tasting Notes

Name of wine:

Producer: Year: Price:

Appearance:

Nose:

Palate:

Conclusions:

Food match:

Name of wine:

Producer: Year: Price:

Appearance:

Nose:

Palate:

Conclusions:

Food match:

Special occasions:
Red wine for parties

There are fewer reds than whites that have the easy-going, refreshing, moderate degree of flavour that make them drink well over a period of time without food. The sort of tannin that makes deep-coloured young reds astringent turns your tongue and gums to leather after a bit. Beaujolais – choose a light Villages wine, only slightly tannic – flows well. Light young Côtes-du-Rhône reds are tolerable, but the sort of cherry-reds such as Valpolicella, Bardolino and Chiaretto of north-east Italy can be better. I stress the 'can'. The tendency in Valpolicella – indeed in most places – is to go for extra weight, and any Valpolicella labelled as 'Ripasso' is not a party wine. I would even be wary of the word 'Reserve', which means stronger, more concentrated – and that's not what you're looking for. In California I would choose a light Zinfandel – not always easy to find – or an aromatic Pinot Noir.

The most valuable role of red wine at parties is in mid-winter, when it becomes the basis for what the British call mulled wine, the Germans *Glühwein*. The principle is simple: red wine mixed with orange and lemon juice (and zest), sweetened with sugar syrup, strengthened (this is optional) with brandy and spiced with cloves and cinnamon. Experience has taught me never to let the mixture boil, and to use an orange liqueur such as Grand Marnier in preference to brandy – added at the last minute. And serve it properly hot. Tepid mulled wine is not nice.

Tasting Notes

Name of wine:

Producer: Year: Price:

Appearance:

Nose:

Palate:

Conclusions:

Food match:

Name of wine:

Producer: Year: Price:

Appearance:

Nose:

Palate:

Conclusions:

Food match:

The most valuable role of red wine
at parties is in mid-winter, when
it becomes the basis for
mulled wine.

Tasting Notes

Name of wine:

Producer: Year: Price:

Appearance:

Nose:

Palate:

Conclusions:

Food match:

Name of wine:

Producer: Year: Price:

Appearance:

Nose:

Palate:

Conclusions:

Food match:

Special occasions:
Fizz for frivolity

The wine purpose-built for parties is Champagne, or any of the countless sparkling wines made in almost every region today, preferably, though not always, by the 'classic method'. The frivolity of fizz is its essential quality. It does not need to be the most expensive brand for a party – any party – even if you can afford it. Great bottles of luxury cuvées deserve to be kept for more intimate occasions.

There are numerous good alternatives to Champagne, at every price, and from virtually every country and region, from New Zealand to England to Chile via California. Italy's Prosecco is reliable and good value, and Spain's Cava fruity and fresh. These two wines are relatively soft in flavour and could be considered for an afternoon party (like many weddings) when very dry Champagne can be out of place. The less dry Champagne alternative, demi-sec, is not usually as good, in my experience, as some of the attractively fruity Crémants (top-quality sparklers) of the Loire, Alsace or Burgundy.

Someone once transferred to sparkling wine the essentially tranquil idea of a great Burgundian priest and war hero, the Canon Kir, who liked his dry, acidic white Aligoté enriched with crème de cassis, the blackcurrant cordial of his home town, Dijon. A 'Kir Royale' is Champagne and cassis. Come to that, a 'King's Peg', regal reviver of jaded professors at Cambridge University (King's College claims the invention) is the same idea only using vintage Champagne and a lovely old pale vintage cognac as its ingredients. A Bucks Fizz is of course Champagne and (freshly squeezed) orange juice, a Bellini peach juice and, correctly, Prosecco.

Tasting Notes

Name of wine:

Producer: Year: Price:

Appearance:

Nose:

Palate:

Conclusions:

Food match:

Name of wine:

Producer: Year: Price:

Appearance:

Nose:

Palate:

Conclusions:

Food match:

When you are on your own half a bottle seems plenty, but when there are two of you one bottle scarcely seems enough.

Tasting Notes

Name of wine:

Producer: Year: Price:

Appearance:

Nose:

Palate:

Conclusions:

Food match:

Name of wine:

Producer: Year: Price:

Appearance:

Nose:

Palate:

Conclusions:

Food match:

If you like this, try this...

Why should wines from different grapes and climates taste alike? Sometimes they just do: there can be similarities of structure, with high acidity or low, with brick-like tannins or supple ones. It doesn't make them interchangeable, and though you may adore the aromas of both Hermitage and Barolo there will still be days when you want one and not the other. Thinking about wines in terms of grapes or regions is not the only way: to think of similarities of flavour and style across continents can make one see wines differently.

If you like Clare Riesling, try Petit and Gros Manseng

The Clare region of Australia has reintroduced Riesling to wine-lovers uncertain about the complications of European Riesling: it has clear, singing flavours of lime cordial and toast, and it ages well, gaining layers of spiced honey without any hint of sweetness. Its high acidity keeps it company while it ages: it's linear, pure, and clean as a whistle. Petit and Gros Manseng are from south-west France: think of limes and apricots, picked ripe, with vibrant acidity. It doesn't age as well as Riesling, but if you love those intense lime-cordial flavours, this is the way to go. Petit Manseng has the more extreme style, and both can be made dry or sweet.

If you like Chablis, try Saar Riesling

Good Chablis is searingly mineral; tight and deceptively light in youth,

Thinking about wines in terms of grapes and regions is not the only way.

Tasting Notes

Name of wine:

Producer: Year: Price:

Appearance:

Nose:

Palate:

Conclusions:

Food match:

Name of wine:

Producer: Year: Price:

Appearance:

Nose:

Palate:

Conclusions:

Food match:

it fills out with age to become immensely complex. It's a terroir wine: never especially fruity, it reflects the chalk and clay, sun and wind of its northerly hills. Saar Riesling is a northern wine, too: the leanest and most intense of German Rieslings, it comes from a chilly tributary of the Mosel, more marginal in climate than the great Mittelmosel yet reaching surprisingly high ripeness levels to balance its taut acidity. A mature Saar Riesling demands one's full attention: its layers of complexity emerge slowly, with smoke and earth, peaches and lemon zest, and the minerality of those breezy German hills.

If you like Grüner Veltliner, try Verdicchio

There's more minerality here too – it's the secret weapon of great dry whites. Grüner Veltliner comes at all levels of ripeness and quality, from light quaffing wines served by the half-litre in Austrian Heurigen, to powerful, structured single-vineyard wines from the best sites of the Wachau and Kamptal. It's not particularly aromatic, but there'll be a note of white pepper and bayleaf there, with some celery and, in the biggest wines, some ripe apricot and peach flavours. The same structure can be found in Verdicchio: it's the wine Italians choose when they want a white wine that reminds them of a red. Verdicchio doesn't boast much aroma; instead there's acidity, weight and a certain nuttiness to balance the quince fruit. Neither it nor Grüner Veltliner are showy: subtle power is what they're about.

If you like Muscat, try Gewürztraminer

There's far less subtlety about these two. Muscat smells and tastes overwhelmingly of grapes: the most aromatic, flower-scented, crunchy grapes you can image. It covers a vast selection of wines, from the lightness of Asti to the caramelised weight of Victorian fortified Muscat from Australia. But imagine something in the middle: something dry or dryish, delicate but not evanescant, perhaps from Italy or Austria; and then imagine a Gewürztraminer from Alsace, all spice and perfume, roses and lychees, probably off-dry but creamy enough to taste off-dry even if it's not; it's a natural step.

Tasting Notes

Name of wine:

Producer: Year: Price:

Appearance:

Nose:

Palate:

Conclusions:

Food match:

Name of wine:

Producer: Year: Price:

Appearance:

Nose:

Palate:

Conclusions:

Food match:

Tasting Notes

Name of wine:

Producer: Year: Price:

Appearance:

Nose:

Palate:

Conclusions:

Food match:

Name of wine:

Producer: Year: Price:

Appearance:

Nose:

Palate:

Conclusions:

Food match:

If you like red burgundy, try Malbec

The fascination of red burgundy is hard to imitate: the incense notes of youth, the mineral spiciness, the perfect focus. Describing Pinot in terms of flavours, be they strawberry or cherry, game or leather, gives very little idea of what it's actually like on the palate. But the flavours of Malbec are not so far away, and the structure is similar, too: acidity, firmness, some silky flesh. If Malbec is overripe, or worked too hard, or overoaked, it can be made into something resembling Frankenstein's monster. We're talking here about light to middleweight Malbec from high-altitude sites in Argentina: elegant, aromatic, and always with that trademark silkiness. There's a strong similarity of style.

If you like red Rioja, try Alentejo

The keynote here is bright red fruit, though with a rounded, friendly profile: red Rioja slips down very, very easily. Tempranillo has the strawberry fruit and the acidity; Garnacha adds some toffee sweetness, and there may be some Mazuelo there for colour, or Graciano for violet perfume. The fruit is more accentuated than in the past: the wines are fresh, concentrated, silky. Portugal's Alentejo is a more recent addition to the repertoire: it produces masses of wine, but only recently has it developed a definite style of its own. And that style is bright, spicy, balanced; not overripe, but pure, fresh and juicy. So far it's not hitting the heights that Rioja at its best can reach, but as an everyday red it should be right on the button for Rioja lovers.

If you like Merlot, try Carmenère

This is a no-brainer, really: for years growers in Chile thought they were the same vine. They were mixed up together in the vineyards, and they look very similar: the differences are as subtle as the colour of the underside of the young leaves. But they ripen at different times, so have to be treated differently. And they taste different. Merlot's flavour can be a little hard to pin down, it's true: anything from lush, juicy and toffeeish in much of the New World to the darkly spicy complexities of Pomerol. But it tends to be low to lowish in acidity, and there's that

Tasting Notes

Name of wine:

Producer: Year: Price:

Appearance:

Nose:

Palate:

Conclusions:

Food match:

Name of wine:

Producer: Year: Price:

Appearance:

Nose:

Palate:

Conclusions:

Food match:

seductive mouthfeel .... Carmenère is low in acidity, too, and has a chocolatey fleshiness to its fruit. There's black-pepper spice there, and the tannins are supple and silky. Some Chilean Carmenère is just too much: carved from American oak and almost impenetrable. Less expensive wines can be a safer bet.

If you like Northern Rhône reds, try Barolo

Great Northern Rhône Syrah tastes wild, almost dangerous: there's something untamed and feral about its gamey spice and herbs. You can taste the granite and the heat of the sun and the herbs of the *garrigue*: Syrah is a potential blockbuster, but a deeply aromatic one. Barolo is not exactly a pussycat, either: its tannins, like those of the Northern Rhône, need careful vinification to domesticate them. And then the aromas are let loose. Barolo smells and tastes of tar and roses, delicate and deep, feminine and macho at the same time. Neither is a wine to be drunk frivolously; they need thought and patience and some game or a rich, dark, beef stew.

Tasting Notes

Name of wine:

Producer: Year: Price:

Appearance:

Nose:

Palate:

Conclusions:

Food match:

Name of wine:

Producer: Year: Price:

Appearance:

Nose:

Palate:

Conclusions:

Food match:

Each wine you open has a different pleasure (or at least a different experience) to offer

Tasting Notes

Name of wine:

Producer: Year: Price:

Appearance:

Nose:

Palate:

Conclusions:

Food match:

Name of wine:

Producer: Year: Price:

Appearance:

Nose:

Palate:

Conclusions:

Food match:

Quick reference vintage charts

These charts give a picture of the range of qualities made in the principal 'classic' areas (every year has its relative successes and failures) and a guide to whether the wine is ready to drink or should be kept. Generalisations are unavoidable.

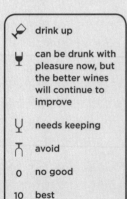

	drink up
	can be drunk with pleasure now, but the better wines will continue to improve
	needs keeping
	avoid
0	no good
10	best

	Germany		Italy		Spain
Vintage	Rhine	Mosel	Piedmont reds	Tuscan reds	Rioja
2010	6–8	6–8	6–8	7–8	7–8
2009	7–9	6–8	7–8	7–8	8–9
2008	6–8	6–8	7–9	7–8	7–8
2007	8–9	8–9	7–9	8–9	7–8
2006	6–7	6–9	8–9	7–10	6–7
2005	8–10	8–10	6–8	5–9	7–8
2004	6–8	6–8	7–9	7–9	7–9
2003	6–9	6–9	6–8	6–8	6–7
2002	7–8	7–8	5–6	5–6	6–7
2001	7–9	8–10	8–9	6–9	7–9
2000	5–8	5–8	7–8	6–7	5–7
1999	7–10	7–10	8–10	8–10	6–7
1998	6–9	6–9	7–8	6–7	7–8

	Australia		Champagne		Port	
Vintage	Shiraz	Chardonnay	Vintage		Vintage	
2010	7–8	7–8	2010	6–7	2010	6–8
2009	7–9	7–8	2009	8–10	2009	7–9
2008	7–8	7–8	2008	8–9	2008	7–8
2007	7–8	7–8	2007	6–7	2007	8–10
2006	7–8	7–8	2006	7–9	2006	6–7
2005	7–9	7–9	2005	7–8	2005	7–8
2004	6–8	6–8	2004	8–9	2004	7–8
2003	5–7	5–7	2003	6–7	2003	8–9
2002	5–8	5–8	2002	8–10	2002	na
2001	6–8	5–7	2001	1–3	2001	6–7
2000	6–8	7–9	2000	7–8	2000	8–10
1999	7–9	5–7	1999	6–8	1999	7–9

	California		New Zealand		S.Africa
Vintage	Cabernet	Chardonnay	Red	White	Red
2010	6–8	6–8	7–9	7–9	7–9
2009	7–9	7–9	7–8	7–9	8–10
2008	6–8	6–8	5–7	7–8	7–8
2007	6–8	7–8	7–8	6–8	7–9
2006	6–8	6–8	6–8	6–8	7–8

France

Vintage	Red Bordeaux		White Bordeaux		Alsace
	Médoc/Graves	Pom/St-Em	Sauternes & sw	Graves & dry	
2010	7–10	6–10	8–10	7–8	8–9
2009	7–10	7–10	8–10	7–9	8–9
2008	6–9	6–9	6–7	7–8	7–8
2007	5–7	6–7	8–9	8–9	6–8
2006	7–8	7–9	8–9	8–9	6–8
2005	9–10	9–10	8–10	8–10	8–9
2004	7–8	7–9	5–7	6–7	6–8
2003	5–9	5–8	7–8	6–7	6–7
2002	6–8	5–8	7–8	7–8	7–8
2001	6–8	7–8	8–10	7–9	6–8
2000	8–10	7–9	6–8	6–8	8–10
1999	5–7	5–8	6–9	7–10	6–8
1998	5–8	6–9	5–8	5–9	7–9
1997	5–7	4–7	7–9	4–7	7–9
1996	6–8	5–7	7–9	7–10	8–10
1995	7–9	6–9	6–8	5–9	6–9
1994	5–8	5–8	4–6	5–8	6–9
1993	4–6	5–7	2–5	5–7	6–8
1992	3–5	3–5	3–5	4–8	5–7

France continued

Vintage	Burgundy			Rhône	
	Côte d'Or red	Côte d'Or white	Chablis	Rhône (N)	Rhône (S)
2010	7–8	6–7	7–9	8–9	7–8
2009	7–10	7–8	7–8	7–9	7–8
2008	7–9	7–9	7–9	6–7	5–7
2007	7–8	8–9	8–9	6–8	7–8
2006	7–8	8–10	8–9	7–8	7–9
2005	7–9	7–9	7–9	7–8	6–8
2004	6–7	7–8	7–8	6–7	6–7
2003	6–7	6–7	6–7	5–7	6–8
2002	7–8	7–8	7–8	4–6	5–5
2001	6–8	7–9	6–8	7–8	7–9
2000	7–8	6–9	7–9	6–8	7–9
1999	7–10	5–7	5–8	7–9	6–9
1998	5–8	5–7	7–8	6–8	7–9
1997	5–8	5–8	7–9	7–9	5–8

Beaujolais 2010, 09, 08, 07. Crus will keep. **Mâcon-Villages** (white). Drink 10, 09, 08. **Loire** (Sweet Anjou and Touraine) best recent vintages: 10, 09, 07, 05, 02, 97, 96, 93, 90, 89; Bourgueil, Chinon, Saumur-Champigny: 10, 09, 06, 05, 04, 02, 00, 99. **Upper Loire (Sancerre, Pouilly-Fumé): 10, 09, 08** Muscadet **10 DYA.**

Winespeak

A

acetic

Unless wine is protected from the oxygen in the air its bacteria will produce volatile acetic acid, giving it a faint taste and smell of vinegar.

acidity

At least half a dozen different acids are essential for zest, liveliness, aroma – the best wines have plenty of acid balanced by plenty of stuffing. You taste too much acid in poor wines because the stuffing is missing.

aftertaste

The flavour that lingers in your mouth after a sip. Scarcely noticeable (and occasionally unpleasant) in a poor wine; deliciously haunting in a great one. (*See caudalie.*)

alcohol

Between 7 and 25 per cent of a wine is alcohol, with most table wines in a range from 10·5 to 13·5 per cent. During fermentation all or some of the sugar in the grapes is converted into ethyl alcohol, which acts as a preservative and gives the wine its 'vinosity', or winey-ness.

amontillado

A matured fino sherry, naturally (and best) dry but often sweetened to be mellow in taste.

AOC

Appellation d'Origine Contrôlée (controlled designation of origin) is the official rank of all the best French wines. On a label, this guarantees both place of origin and a certain style – though not, of course, quality. Shortened to *Appellation Contrôlée* (AC).

aroma

The primary smell of a young wine, compounded of grape juice, fermentation and (sometimes) the oak of a barrel.

astringent

Dry quality, causing the mouth to pucker – the result of high tannin or acid content.

Auslese

German for 'selection'. Refers to a category of QmP (*qv*) white wine made of grapes selected for ripeness above a statutory level, depending on the region.

B

balance

The all-important ratio between the different characteristics of a wine, such as fruitiness, sweetness, acidity, tannin content and alcoholic strength. These should harmonise like the various sounds in a symphony.

barrel

A vital part of the stabilising and early ageing process for most of the world's best wines. New oak barrels are now routinely used for adding the strong scent of oak to 'premium' wines – not always with entirely happy results.

Beerenauslese

German for 'grape selection'. A category of QmP (*qv*) wine, sweeter and more expensive than Auslese because only the ripest bunches are used. Ages admirably.

beeswing

A kind of deposit sometimes found in port, so called because of the veined pattern it forms.

Bereich

A large area, although smaller than a 'region', in Germany. Bernkastel and Johannisberg are *Bereich* (as well as village) names, increasing the quantity of wine available under these names – but doing nothing for its quality.

bin

A section of a cellar devoted to one wine – hence 'bin-ends' for oddments on sale.

bitterness

A taste not usually found in good wines – although some young tannins can be bitter – but a characteristic aftertaste of many north-west Italian wines.

blend

Nearly every wine involves some blending, whether it be of grapes, vintages, or the contents of different vats. With fortified wines blending is almost universal. But blends of wines from different regions or countries tend to lack a distinctive character. (Some Australian blenders would disagree.)

bodega

Spanish word meaning a large storage vault, a wine-producing establishment or a bar.

Botrytis cinerea

The so-called 'noble rot', a mould that has the effect of concentrating the sugar and flavouring substances in grapes by allowing the evaporation of the water in the juice. Under controlled conditions it is used to produce sweet white wines of the highest quality (for example in Tokaji and Sauternes).

bottle-age

The length of time a wine has been kept in bottle (rather than in cask).

bottle-sickness

A (usually) temporary setback in a wine's flavour for weeks or months after bottling.

bottle-stink

A bad smell, which almost instantly dissipates, sometimes found on opening old bottles.

Bottle-stink can be confused with 'corkiness' – but only for a few minutes.

bouquet
The characteristic smell of a matured wine, by analogy with a posy of flowers. Strictly speaking not the same as aroma (*qv*).

breathing
What wine is doing when you expose it to the air by decanting it a few hours before drinking. Opinions are divided as to whether it benefits. *See pages 42–3.*

brut
Extremely dry. Usually used only in connection with Champagne.

bunch thinning
The selective removal of some of the ripening grapes in order to concentrate the flavour and colour of the remaining crop.

C

carafe
Stopperless container used for serving wine at table. The 'carafe wine' ('jug wine' in the US) in a restaurant is the standard house wine.

cask
Another term for a wooden barrel used for storing wine or spirit. A sherry cask is a 'butt'; a port cask is a 'pipe'.

caudalie
French measure of the length of time the aftertaste of a wine lasts.

cave
French for cellar.

chambrer
French word meaning to bring (wine) from cellar- to room-temperature. *See pages 40–41.*

chaptalisation
The French term for the addition of a small permitted amount of sugar during fermentation in order to boost the alcoholic strength of a wine.

character
Term of praise indicating that a wine has its own distinctive and individual stamp.

château
Used in a wine context, this means either the country house or mansion of a wine-producing estate or the estate as a whole. Where it appears on a French label it means that the wine comes solely from that estate.

château-bottled
Bottled on the estate rather than by the merchant. Château-bottled wines are generally more highly valued, whether or not their quality justifies it.

claret

English term for the red wines of Bordeaux.

classé

French word meaning 'classed'. Each important area of France has its own 'classed growths', but there is no unifying system. The term is most often used about Bordeaux.

classico

Italian for 'classic', referring to the core of a DOC (*qv*) region. *Metodo classico* on sparkling wine is the legal term for what used to be called 'Champagne method'.

climat

Burgundian word for an individual vineyard site.

commune

The French for parish. Many wines bear the name of a parish rather than that of an individual grower (for example St-Julien, St-Emilion, Pommard)

cooperage

A general term for wooden containers or the workshop where they are produced. A cooper is a barrel-maker (and a rich man these days).

corkage

Charge made by a restaurant to those who bring their own wine.

corky or corked

Wine contaminated by a rotten cork, resulting in an unpleasant smell and taste.

coulant

'Flowing'. French term for easy-to-drink wines such as Beaujolais.

coulure

A condition of the vine at flowering time, causing the grapes to fall off prematurely.

cradle

A device for holding a bottle in a near-horizontal position so that it can be opened and poured without the deposit being disturbed, properly used only for decanting purposes. The basket fulfils a similar function.

crémant

Now a controlled French appellation for the sparkling wines of certain quality regions, notably the Loire, Alsace and Burgundy.

cru

French word for 'growth', applied to the produce of a vineyard or group of vineyards making wine of a particular character.

crust

A heavy deposit found particularly in bottles of vintage port.

cuvée

The contents of a *cuve* (vat). It can also mean a quantity of blended wine.

D

decant

To transfer wine from a bottle to a stoppered flask (decanter). *See pages 42–3.*

demi-sec

French for 'half-dry'. Usually applied to sparkling wines, the term means that sugar has been added to produce a degree of sweetness, sometimes marked.

deposit

High-quality wines maturing in bottle often develop a greater or lesser deposit, the fall-out from chemical changes which give them greater character, complexity and bouquet.

DOC

Denominazione di Origine Controllata (controlled denomination of origin) is an Italian classification, similar to the French AOC (*qv*) but here more a bureaucratic control than an assurance of quality.

DOCG

The top category of Italian wines, theoretically superior to DOC (*qv*) as indicated by the addition of the letter G for *garantita* (guaranteed).

domaine

A (wine-producing) property. This is the normal word in Burgundy, whereas in Bordeaux they use the term 'château'.

dosage

The sweetening added to sparkling wine before the final corking.

dry

A relative term, implying the opposite of sweet.

E

Einzellage

German term meaning a single, individual vineyard site, as opposed to a *Grosslage* (*qv*), which refers to a collection of such sites.

Eiswein

Very sweet German wine made by harvesting frozen grapes during a frost and pressing them while they are still frozen. The flavours and acidity are intensely concentrated and the wine apparently almost immortal.

éleveur

Someone who buys new wine from the grower and prepares it (or 'brings it up') for sale.

Erzeugerabfüllung

Literally 'producer-bottling'. The German equivalent of 'domaine-bottled'.

extract

Soluble solids from the grape which contribute to the weight and fullness of a wine: the components of its flavour.

F

Fass

German for cask.

fermentation

The conversion of grape juice into wine through the action of certain yeasts present on the skins which turn sugar into alcohol. *See also* malolactic fermentation.

fine

A general term of approbation denoting overall quality.

fining

Clarifying wine by pouring on a coagulant (such as egg whites) and letting it settle.

finish

The final taste left by a sip of wine on swallowing.

fino

The finest style of sherry – dry, delicate and usually light in colour. Finos should be drunk as fresh as possible, and never kept in an opened bottle.

fliers

Little specks of sediment.

fortified

Strengthened by the addition of extra alcohol during production.

foxy

Tasting of native American or 'fox' grapes.

frais

French term meaning either fresh or cool.

frappé

French for very cold or iced.

frizzante

An Italian term meaning slightly sparkling, as opposed to *spumante* which is fully sparking.

fruity

Tasting pleasantly of ripe grapes – but a term so widely used as to have little clear meaning.

full or full-bodied

Refers to a wine that is high in alcohol and extract, causing it to feel weighty and substantial in the mouth.

fumé

Literally 'smoky'. The term refers to the tangy aroma of certain young wines made from the Sauvignon Blanc, for example Pouilly Fumé.

fût
General French word for a cask.

G

gazéifié
French for fizzy or carbonated.

generic
In California, the opposite of 'varietal', for example wine called 'Burgundy' or 'Chablis' is 'generic', while those labelled 'Pinot Noir' and 'Chardonnay' are 'varietal'.

Grand Cru
Literally 'great growth'. In Burgundy it means the top rank. In Bordeaux almost everything is a 'Grand Cru'. In South Africa, for some reason, it can refer to a cheap white wine.

Grosslage
In German terminology a group of neighbouring *Einzellages* (*qv*) of supposedly similar character.

H

hock
Now archaic British term for the white wines of the Rhine and surrounding areas.

hybrid
Used in wine circles of a cross between French and American vines, designed for hardiness. Hybrids are much used in the eastern USA. .

J

jug wine
Otherwise known as 'carafe wine', '*vin ordinaire*' or 'plonk'. Cheap, workaday wine without pretensions.

K

Kabinett
The first category of *Qualitätswein mit Prädikat*, the highest classification of German wine. Kabinett wines are lighter and less expensive than other QmP (*qv*) wines such as Spätlese and Auslese.

Kellerabfüllung
Bottled at the (German) cellar.

L

lagar
The stone trough in which the grapes are (or were) trodden by barefoot workers to make port and other Portuguese wines.

Lage
German term for a particular vineyard.

lees
Solid residue remaining in the cask after the wine has been drawn off.

legs
The rivulets that run down the side of a wine glass after the wine has been swirled around

it. When the legs are pronounced it indicates a wine rich in body and extract.

light
Possessing a low degree of alcohol or, more loosely, lacking in body. Desirable in some cases, most German wines for example, but not where something more intense is required.

liquorous
Used of wine that is rich, sweet and pretty strong. In French, *liquoreux*. Sauternes is the classic example.

M

maderized
The term refers to the brown colour and flat taste of a white wine that has been over-exposed to air during production or maturation to the extent that it smells or tastes like Madeira.

malolactic fermentation
A secondary stage of fermentation in which malic acid is converted into lactic acid and carbon dioxide. As lactic acid is milder, the taste of the wine becomes less acid. Some winemakers encourage it by warming the new wine. Others avoid it to keep a sharper acidity.

marc
The pulpy mass of grape skins and pips left after the fermented grapes have been pressed.

Also the name of the strong-smelling brandy distilled from this.

marque
French for brand. In Champagne the '*grandes marques*' are the top dozen or so houses.

méthode champenoise
The 'Champagne method'. Formerly used world-wide to signify the laborious way of making sparkling wine perfected in Champagne, but now outlawed in favour of the words 'classic method' or local equivalents.

millésime
French for the vintage year (for example 1998).

mise
French word meaning 'putting', used for bottling. The past participle occurs in such phrases as *mis en bouteille au château* (château-bottled). *Mise du château* means the same thing.

moelleux
French for 'marrow-like'. Used of a wine it means soft and rich, particularly of Loire wines such as Vouvray that vary from dry one year to *moelleux* the next.

monopole
A wine whose brand name is the exclusive property of a particular firm or grower.

mousseux
French for sparkling. Not usually used for first-class wines.

N

négociant
French term loosely translated as 'shipper', but implying a dealer who buys wine from the estates and distributes it wholesale or retail.

nerveux
A term of praise implying fineness combined with firmness and vitality.

noble rot
See Botrytis cinerea.

nose
Wine jargon for smell, whether aroma or bouquet (*qqv*).

nouveau
As in Beaujolais Nouveau – the wine of the last harvest, in its first winter.

O

oaky
Refers to a wine that has picked up something of the taste and smell of the oak cask in which it was matured.

oeil de perdrix
'Eye of the partridge', used to describe the

pink colour of certain rosé wines, some pink Champagnes and whites with a pinkish tinge.

oenology
Knowledge or study of wine (from the Greek *oinos*, wine).

oenophile
A lover or connoisseur of wines.

oloroso
A natural style of sherry classified as 'pungent' (as opposed to 'fine'). With age it becomes the noblest, nuttiest, most memorable of all.

Originalabfüllung
The German equivalent of *mis en bouteille au château*. It means 'original bottling' and signifies that the wine has been bottled on the premises by the grower. *Originalabzug* means the same.

oxidised
Possessing a stale, flat taste owing to excessive exposure to air. *See also* maderized.

P

palo cortado
A rare and excellent style of sherry, between fino and oloroso (*qqv*).

passito, vino
Strong, sweet Italian dessert wine made from

grapes that are dried for a brief period before being pressed.

pasteurisation

Process invented by Louis Pasteur (1822–95) in which substances are sterilised by heat. It is used for certain run-of-the-mill wines, but it is not considered desirable for the finer ones.

pelure d'oignon

Onion skin. This is how the French describe the pale, orange-brown colour of certain rosé wines and some old reds.

perlant

Showing a slight degree of sparkle, much less than *mousseux* (*qv*).

Perlwein

German name for a wine that is *pétillant*.

pétillant

Having a very light, natural sparkle, even less pronounced than that of a *perlant* wine.

phylloxera

An American vine pest accidentally introduced into Europe in the late 19th century which destroyed almost all vineyards, not only in Europe but throughout the world, in a disaster without precedent. Most vines world-wide are now grafted onto American phylloxera-resistant stock.

pied

French for a single vine.

pipe

A port cask containing 522·48 litres (115 gallons). The word is also used to refer to a Madeira cask containing 418 litres (92 gallons) and a Marsala cask holding 422 litres (92$\frac{2}{3}$ gallons).

plastering

Not getting someone drunk, but boosting the acid content of a wine by the addition of calcium sulphate (plaster of Paris). The practice is more common in Mediterranean countries (especially in making sherry) where the natural acid content of the wine tends to be low.

port

English name for the fortified wine (red and white) produced on the banks of the Douro River in northern Portugal and matured in the cellars at Vila Nova de Gaia. It is made in both red and white forms.

porón

Double-spouted Spanish drinking vessel which enables the wine to be drunk without the glass touching the lips. When the glass is raised one spout lets out a stream of wine while the other lets out air.

pot
A type of fat-bellied wine bottle.

pourriture noble
See Botrytis cinerea.

Prädikat
See QmP.

Premier Cru
First of the five categories of Médoc châteaux established by the classification set up in 1855 which comprises Château Lafite-Rothschild, Château Latour, Château Mouton-Rothschild, Château Margaux and Château Haut-Brion. In Burgundy the term refers to the second grade of classed vineyard (the first is Grand Cru).

premium
California term for wines over a certain fairly modest price – the opposite of 'jug'.

pricked
A useful, if archaic, term for the unpleasantly sharp quality caused by the presence in the wine of too much volatile acidity.

primeur
Term applied to certain wines sold very young, especially Beaujolais.

punt
The hollow mound poking up inside the bottom of a wine bottle. Universal in old hand-blown bottles but now generally limited to Champagne and port.

Q
QbA
Qualitätswein eines bestimmten Anbaugebietes (quality wine from a specific region) is the second-highest category of German wine. QbA wines are made of grapes that ripened insufficiently to make wine without added sugar – as distinct from QmP (*qv*) wines.

QmP
Qualitätswein mit Prädikat (quality wine with special attributes), the top category of German wine, made with only fully ripe grapes. QmP wines are subdivided into five further categories: Kabinett (light and usually fairly dry), Spätlese (fuller and usually fairly sweet), Auslese (rich and usually sweet, sometimes superbly honeyed), Beerenauslese and Trockenbeerenauslese (*qqv*).

R
racking
Transferring the fermented wine from one cask to another to separate it from its lees (*qv*).

ratafia
Brandy mixed with sweet unfermented grape juice, also available as Pineau des Charentes. A speciality of Champagne.

186

récolte
French word for the harvest, crop or vintage.

remuage
Technique invented by the widow Cliquot in the early 19th century for removing the deposit in Champagne without removing the sparkle. It involves shaking and turning each bottle and inclining it at a progressively sharp angle until it is almost upside down. This goes on for six weeks or more until all the deposit has settled on the cork. Then the cork is taken out and the deposit extracted.

reserva
Italian term for wine that has been aged for a

statutory period, its length depending on the DOC (*qv*).

réserve
An uncontrolled French term implying superior quality.

riserva
Spanish equivalent of *reserva* (*qv*). *Gran riserva* is the highest official category.

rosato
Italian for rosé.

rosé
Pink wine made from black grapes pressed

quickly to allow only some of the skin-colour to tinge the wine. Rosés vary in colour from deep pink, almost red, to pale, almost white.

rosso
Italian for red.

rouge
French for red.

ruby
Young red port, darker and fruitier than tawny, that has aged in wood for two to three years.

rurale, méthode
Probably the original way of making sparkling wine, antedating the *méthode champenoise*. Still used, with modifications, in Limoux in south-west France.

S

sack
Archaic term for sherry and similar wines.

Schaumwein
German for sparkling wine. No implication of quality.

Schillerwein
A type of German rosé wine, made from a mixture of black and white grapes. The name comes from the word *Schilller* meaning lustre, and has nothing to do with the poet Schiller.

Schoppenwein
The 'open' wine sold in a German *Weinstube* or tavern.

sec
In French this word means dry or fermented out, but in relation to Champagne it is used in a specialised way. A very dry Champagne is described as *brut*. *Sec* means it contains some added sweetness. *Demi-sec* (*qv*) means decidedly sweet. With other wines *sec* is an indication of relative rather than absolute dryness. The same applies to the Italian *secco*.

sediment
Solid matter deposited in a bottle in the course of the maturing process. Nearly always a good sign.

Sekt
The German word for sparkling wine.

solera
The name for a system of blending and maturing sherry, also applied to the storage building where the process takes place. The sherry is arranged in different casks according to age and character, and the contents of the casks are transferrred and blended.

sommelier
French term for a wine waiter.

sparkling

Containing bubbles of carbon dioxide gas. This condition can be brought about in three different ways: (1) fermentation in the bottle (Champagne or 'classic' method); (2) fermentation in a closed vat (Charmat method); (3) pumping CO_2 into the wine (rudely called the Bicycle Pump method).

Spätlese

German term for a wine made from late-harvested grapes.

spritzer

A drink made with white wine diluted with soda or mineral water.

spritzig

German adjective describing a wine with a light, natural sparkle.

spumante

Italian for fully sparkling.

sulphur

The most common disinfectant for wine. It is dusted onto the vines to prevent fungus, burnt inside casks to fumigate them and added to the must, usually in the form of sulphur dioxide, to destroy harmful bacteria.

süss

German for sweet.

Süssreserve

Unfermented, and therefore naturally sweet, grape juice. Used in Germany to blend with dry wines to balance them.

T

table wine

In common use, this means any non-fortified wine. In EC terms it means a wine below the rank of *Vin de Qualité Produit dans une Région Déterminée* or VQPRD (*qv*).

Tafelwein

Deutscher Tafelwein is the lowest of the three categories of German wine. '*Deutscher*' indicates that the wine is made entirely in Germany. If it is called simply *Tafelwein* it may be blended with wines from other countries.

tannin

A substance found in the skins, stalks and pips of grapes. It is also absorbed into wine from oak casks and is sometimes added artificially. Tannin acts as a preservative and is therefore an important ingredient if the wine is to be matured over a long period. In excess it imparts a hard, dry quality. But fine ripe tannins contribute the essential, satisfying, 'structure' of a wine in the mouth.

tartaric

An acid occurring naturally in grapes and the main constituent of the acidity in wine.

tastevin

Shallow vessel of silver, glass or ceramic, used in Burgundy for sampling wine. Its shape makes it easier to judge the colour of a wine in a dark cellar.

tawny

The name given to port that has been aged in wood until it has acquired a tawny colour.

terroir

A French word meaning soil and site in their ecological totality. A wine is said to have *un goût de terroir* (a taste of the soil) when it has gathered certain nuances of taste and flavour from the land on which it was produced.

tête de cuvée

A term used mainly in the Burgundy area to refer to the 'cream' of the wine sold under a particular name.

tinto

Spanish for red.

tirage

French word usually meaning the transfer of wine from cask to bottle. Literally 'drawing off'.

Tischwein

German for table wine. Not an official term (see *Tafelwein*) but used to refer to ordinary mealtime wines.

trocken

German for dry. Trocken wines are often good with food in the QbA and Spätlese categories.

Trockenbeerenauslese (TBA)

A category of German wine. It is made by picking out individual grapes affected by the noble rot, *Botrytis cinerea*, which produce an exceptionally rich, luscious wine.

U

ullage

The amount of wine needed to top up a bottle (or barrel) right to the cork. 'Ullaged' bottles (with empty necks) can be disappointing.

V

varietal

A varietal wine is one that is named after the grape variety from which it is made. 'Varietal' is an adjective, 'variety' the noun.

vat

Large vessel or tank for fermenting or blending wine. Nowadays vats may be made of wood, concrete or stainless steel, sometimes with a glass lining.

VDQS

(*Vin Délimité de Qualité Supérieur*) The second official category of French wines, subject to slightly less rigorous regulations than those applying to *Appellation Contrôlée* wines.

vendange
The French word for vintage.

vendemmia
The Italian word for vintage.

vignoble
French for vineyard.

vin de garde
A wine whose potential to mature makes it worth keeping.

vin de l'année
Literally 'wine of the year', that is to say of the current vintage.

vin de la région
What you ask for when you want a wine made in the region where you happen to be.

vin de liqueur
This is the French name for what in Britain would be called 'fortified wine', a term which in France would imply an improper addition of alcohol.

vin de paille
A (now rare) way of producing sweet wine with a mild but fresh and lively taste by drying the grapes on straw *(paille)* mats before crushing and fermenting them.

vin de pays
Not to be confused with *vin de la région*, this is the third official category of French wines. The wines are now innumerable, some large *(vin de pays de zone)*, some covering *départements* *(vin de pays départementale)*, some (the most interesting) small districts.

Vin Doux Naturel
(VDN). A description used for a type of wine made in southern France, high in natural sugar and fortified by the addition of extra alcohol. Drink them as dessert wines, after meals or on their own, like sherry.

vin jaune
These are white wines with a yellowish hue caused by bacterial action during the long fermentation process. Made solely in the Jura region of France, they have a strong and distinctive flavour and bouquet.

vin nouveau
New wine, made to be drunk just after the vintage. Beaujolais is the most famous, but many other French regions market a *nouveau*.

vin ordinaire
Not an official category of French wine but a loose term for basic wine regarded as a grocery commodity, not a subject for connoisseurship.

viña
Spanish for vineyard.

vinho generoso
Spanish term for aperitif and dessert wines such as sherry.

vinho verde
Light, tangy wine made in northern Portugal. The name, meaning 'green wine', refers to its newness, not its colour. It comes in both red and white.

vintage
The annual harvesting and production of a wine. More particularly, a vintage wine is one that bears the date of the vintage on the label, either because it is meant to be drunk young or because it was made to be matured over a number of years.

viticulture
The science and art of growing grapes.

VQPRD
Vin de Qualité Produit dans une Région Déterminée (quality wine produced in a defined zone). This is an EC quality category. Italian DOC, French AOC and German QbA (*qqv*) wines all qualify.

W

Weingut
Term used in Germany and Austria for a wine-producing estate that grows its own grapes.

Weissherbst
A type of white wine made in Baden, Germany, from black grapes.

Winzergenossenschaft
The German word for a wine cooperative, a group of growers who have clubbed together to produce wine.

Y

yeast
A collection of micro-organisms that cause fermentation (*qv*). Wild yeasts are naturally present on grape skins, but artificially developed yeasts are used by most modern winemakers (except the best).

yield
The amount of wine produced by a vineyard, usually expressed in hectolitres (100 litres) per hectare or hl/ha. Higher quantity means lower quality or lighter wine that matures more rapidly.

Acknowledgements

Picture credits:

Alamy: Bon Appetit/Klaus Arras 110–11; Michelle
Chaplow 122; David Noton Photography 186;
georgina 78; Johner Images/Hans Geijer
142–3; numb 88–9; Payless Images, Inc. 82–3;
PhotoAlto/Isabelle Rozenbaum 23 right; Richard
Semik 20; Peter Titmuss 52–3
Corbis: Dave Bartruff 108; Doug Berry 4–5;
Owen Franken 72; Image Source 6; C. Lyttle
62; moodboard 13; Sudres/photocuisine 68;
Tetra Images 45; the food passionates/Nicholas
Lemonnier 98
Fotolia: fotum 145; Kay Ransom 152
Gap Interior Images: House & Leisure/W. Heath 48
Getty Images: Giannis Agelou 126–7; Anthony-
Masterton 66; Assembly 91; Maren Caruso 9;
Fuse 19; Andrea Gomez 86; Image Source 168;
Ray Kachatorian 150; Luna 94; Ian O'Leary 14;
Dean Sanderson 58; Teubner/StockFood Creative
43; Carl Tremblay 164; Barry Wong 137
Hugh Johnson 51, 146
Masterfile 32
Octopus Publishing Group: 38–9; Russell Sadur 47
Photolibrary.com: 174; Corbis 25; Fancy 74–5;
Hammond/SoFood Collection 37; Image Source
23 left; Lite Productions/Glow Images RF 29;
White Star/Monica Gumm/Imagebroker.net 114
Rex Features: INS News Agency Ltd 30
Thinkstock: Comstock 116–17; Stockbyte 27